FURNITURE
FIX-UPS

FURNITURE FIX-UPS

75 Easy Ideas for Fresh New Looks

Country
Sampler
B O O K S

Country Sampler Books is an imprint of Emmis Books.

For further information, contact the publisher at

Emmis Books
1700 Madison Road
Cincinnati, OH 45206
www.emmisbooks.com

Library of Congress Cataloging-in-Publication Data

Furniture fix-ups: easy ideas for fresh new looks/by the editors of Country Sampler.
        p. cm. -- (From drab to fab)
  Includes index.
  ISBN-13: 978-1-57860-225-4
  ISBN-10: 1-57860-225-4
  1. Furniture--Repairing. 2. Furniture finishing. 3. Used furniture.
I. Country Sampler (St. Charles, Ill.) II. Series.
  TT199.F79 2005
  645'.4--dc22

                        200500978

Edited by Lisa Sloan

Designed by Catherine LePenske

Introduction

There's nothing *Country Sampler Decorating Ideas* readers like better than learning how to transform timeworn furnishings into work-of-art pieces. In this book, you'll find more than 75 ways to turn trash into treasure, form new furniture from old stuff and convert unfinished wood pieces into custom-colored accents. We've compiled our readers' favorite furniture projects from past issues of *Country Sampler Decorating Ideas* magazine and show you how to recreate them at home. Step-by-step instructions, tried-and-true techniques and how-to photos guide you as you rejuvenate and fix up your own furniture.

Hope you enjoy the book,

Ann Wilson

Ann Wilson,
Editor of *Country Sampler
Decorating Ideas*

CONTENTS

28

12

38

52

80

68

100

114

Some Terms to Know

▲ CRACKLE

CRACKLE—A medium applied between a base coat and top coat that causes the top coat to shrink and crack, revealing the base color, for an aged look.

DECOUPAGE MEDIUM—A medium used to glue cutout paper images to surfaces; it also acts as a sealer.

DRY BRUSHING—Softly tinting a previously painted surface using a brush with just a small amount of a different-color paint on the tips of the bristles.

FLORAL SPRAY PAINT—A sheer, fast-drying spray paint used by florists and crafters to tint flowers, it can also be used to apply layers of color to furniture.

GLAZE BASE—A clear medium designed to be tinted by mixing with paint. Used for many faux finishes, it is semitransparent; the more glaze in the mixture, the more translucent the result. It also extends the drying time of paint.

ROTTENSTONE—A decomposed limestone material used to give furniture an aged look. The gray, mildly abrasive powder is also used as a polishing agent for wood finishes and some metallic surfaces.

Brushes and Tools

ARTIST BRUSHES—Small brushes used by artists that come in many shapes, including flat, round and angled, and are great for adding details and touching up.

BURNISHING TOOL—A plastic pan scraper or credit card used to smooth decoupaged cutouts and press out bubbles and excess glue.

CHIP BRUSH—Also called China bristle brush, an inexpensive natural bristle paintbrush used to apply glaze. Its bristles leave brush marks and can be used to create interesting patterns.

COMBING TOOLS—Flat rubber or metal tools with notched edges (or teeth) used to create patterns when pulled through paint or glaze.

PAINTERS TAPE—Specialty low-tack tape available in various widths. It is used to protect areas from paint and mask off patterns, like stripes or borders. Remove tape before paint is completely dry for best results.

ROCKER-STYLE WOOD-GRAINING TOOL—A tool with a molded rubber surface used to produce a realistic pattern of the heart grain of wood.

SHAPER TOOLS—Rubber- or silicone-tipped tools that come in various shapes, sizes and levels of firmness. They are used to carve images in wet paint or glaze.

TRANSFER PAPER—A pigment-backed product that works like carbon paper to transfer a design from one surface to another. Transfer paper is placed ink-side down on the surface with the pattern on top, then the pattern lines are traced to transfer the design. (This is different than the photocopy image transfer paper that is used in the Instant Artistry chapter.)

Rummage through your vanity cabinet and you'll find helpful painting tools disguised as beauty aids.

A. EYE SHADOW—
Add shimmering shading to porous surfaces. (Must be sealed to be permanent.)

B. TOOTHBRUSH—
Spatter paint on surfaces or add texture through pouncing.

C. EMERY BOARDS—
Great for detail sanding.

D. COTTON BALLS—
Wipe off excess paint and glaze.

E. MAKEUP BRUSH—
Soften or shade paint on surfaces for detail work.

F. LIP BALM—
A quick way to mask off mirrors or glass instead of using tape.

G. LOOFAH—
A exfoliator with superior sponge-painting ability.

H. COTTON SWABS—
Good for detail work or making small circles or dots with paint.

I. NAIL POLISH REMOVER—
With a cotton ball, test for a varnish or polyurethane finish on wood pieces. (If the finish is varnish, cotton fibers will stick to the surface.)

J. MAKEUP SPONGES—
Handy wedges make perfect substitutes for stencil pouncers.

TIP: *When mixing a glaze or wash, do so in a resealable plastic container to keep it from drying out.*

PRACTICE MAKES PERFECT

Before you set to work on your furniture, practice all techniques on a test board. This not only ensures you are comfortable applying the finish and working with the tools, but also provides an opportunity to try out and adjust paint-to-glaze ratios. It also allows you to check color combinations. Make the test board from a piece of foamboard or from a piece of wood similar to that of your furniture surface. Prepare the test board in the same manner as you would prepare the furniture, applying any necessary primer, base-coating, etc.

A NOTE ABOUT PAINT

All of our projects are done with latex or water-based paints, such as craft acrylics. While many decorative painters prefer to work with alkyd or oil-based products because they have a longer drying time, which allows more time to manipulate the finish, we recommend latex because it offers easier cleanup and less fumes. When you need to extend the dry time of latex paint for a project, we recommend adding glaze or a clear paint conditioner. We recommend using water-based sealers as well.

TIP: *Cleaning up small spills and splatters of water-based paint is child's play if you keep a tub of inexpensive baby wipes handy. Great for quick general cleanup or on hands for stubborn paint removal, baby wipes contain alcohol, which acts as a solvent, breaking down the binder in water-based paint so the pigment can be lifted off. Grab a baby wipe to clean up smears and smudges on your painted surface. It's best to catch the problem while the paint is still wet, but in many cases, you can use wipes to partially remove dried paint.*

Picking Pieces

Carefully select each piece and decide how to paint it based on its personality. Whether you choose to work with a new dresser or a battered old flea market chair, keep these things in mind:

■ Look for a well-proportioned piece that is solid and has a stable construction. Look beyond outdated finishes and replaceable or repairable components, but don't choose a piece with water or other surface damage that has lifted the veneer. Loose or raised veneer must be removed and the scars repaired, a job best left to a professional.

■ Give a piece in good condition a smooth, high-gloss paint treatment to show off its solid, even quality. Don't give a high-shine treatment to pieces with dents, scratches, water damage or cigarette burns. These pieces require a distressed finish or painted designs to distract from imperfections.

■ Feel free to use creative paint treatments on any piece, with the exception of serious antiques. Antiques with original paint should be left intact because original paint, no matter how worn, adds to an antique's value and authenticity.

SAFETY FIRST

PLEASE READ all manufacturer's instructions for proper usage of products before beginning. Work in a well-ventilated area and wear a dust mask or goggles, if needed. Because paints and some cleaning solvents can irritate the skin, wear protective gloves. Protect your work surface with drop cloths, newspaper, kraft paper or strips of cardboard.

Preparation Pointers

POOR SURFACE PREPARATION can doom your project to failure, so make sure you don't skimp on these steps. Start by removing any drawers, cabinet doors and all knobs and make sure you have a clean, dry, smooth surface. Remove dirt and grime by wiping down the piece with a damp cloth. Wash with soap and water and use a degreaser, if needed. Be sure to rinse away any residue.

A FEW SMALL REPAIRS

NOW'S THE TIME to make any basic repairs, such as gluing loose joints with carpenters wood glue and filling in any holes, dents or deep scratches using wood putty. Apply wood putty with a putty knife, then let dry. Sand until the surface is smooth. (If you plan to stain or dye the surface, add a bit of the colorant to the putty before applying it to your piece; dry putty will not absorb the stain or dye the same as the wood and will affect the finished look.)

UNFINISHED WOOD SURFACES

SAND ALL PIECES lightly following the grain, beginning with 120-grit sandpaper and progressing to 220-grit sandpaper. Pay special attention to areas that have end grain. Sand with the grain of the wood on flat surfaces and across the end grain in curved areas. Wipe off all sanding dust with a tack cloth. If you are staining or dying your piece, a clean surface is important—dust particles on the wood may cause uneven color and texture. If you are painting, prime the piece. (Water-based primers and paint may raise the grain of unfinished wood. Lightly sand between coats with 400-grit sandpaper to smooth raised grain.)

PREVIOUSLY FINISHED SURFACES

IF YOU'RE WORKING with a piece that's previously been painted, follow the paint manufacturer's instructions for surface preparation, which may vary depending on the preexisting finish. Although all projects will require at least a light sanding, you'll rarely need to strip an old piece back to bare wood. Stripping is a long, messy process; in most cases it is adequate to sand or strip off just enough of the existing finish to provide a smooth, matte surface that will allow the new paint to bond. After cleaning the piece, gently scrape away any loose or peeling paint. Give pieces the fingernail test—scratch the existing varnish with your fingernail. If the finish is marked or lifted, you'll need to scrape it off with a paint scraper and sand it smooth with fine-grade sandpaper. If your finish has a high-gloss or plastic laminate finish, it will require heavier sanding to rough up the surface to help paint adhere. Always sand with the grain and wipe the surface with a tack cloth to remove the sanding dust.

PRIMING

WOOD IS POROUS and must be primed to prevent pigment from penetrating (except when you will be using a stain or dye; in these cases, you want the product to soak into the raw wood). For some previously painted, stained or varnished pieces, consider a stain-blocking primer to prevent the old color from bleeding through the new finish. (Surfaces such as metal and plastic laminate require special primers; check with your paint dealer.) Apply primer and paint by the same method—if the piece is plain with flat surfaces, apply both primer and paint with a brush or roller. If the furniture has spindles, intricate trim or detailed carvings, you may wish to use a spray primer and paint. Apply primer swiftly and do not redo areas. Primer sets and dries quickly, so reworking may mar the surface.

CLEANUP

To get the maximum use from your brushes, be sure to clean them properly after every project, following the paint manufacturer's instructions. Latex paint can usually be washed off in warm running water. Use a flat-bladed knife to scrape off most of the paint before rinsing. As you rinse, gently separate the bristles and be sure to work on the base of the brush. You may need to add some mild detergent, but be sure to thoroughly rinse. When the brush is clean, give it a few good shakes to fluff up the bristles. Clean rollers and pads the same way, but roll excess paint onto newspaper before rinsing.

TIP: *Loosen dried acrylic or latex paint from a paintbrush by soaking it in hair conditioner or fabric softener.*

PATTERN *Play*

16

18

20

22

HEN IT COMES TO DECORATING, pattern really packs a wallop. It's essential to defining the style of a space—just think of country's cozy checks and florals or the bold geometrics of a contemporary interior. Plus, it's just plain fun to experiment with pattern, no matter what your skill level. Though fabric might seem the natural way to introduce pattern, painted furniture can make an equally strong statement. Start out with stamped or stenciled motifs or use painters tape to make stripes, checks and plaids. Pick up a painting tool, such as a comb or roller, to produce waves, dots or other designs.

ROLL-ON *Gingham*

1. Base-coat chair with sky blue paint and let dry.

2. Mix one part white paint with two parts glaze base. (The glaze mixture must be translucent enough to show a color difference when layering coats.) On a blue-painted test board, paint a stripe, let dry and paint another stripe that intersects the first. The color value should be lighter at the intersection. Adjust the paint-to-glaze ratio if necessary.

3. Using a pencil and quilters ruler, mark guidelines for vertical 1⅛-inch stripes (the width of the stencil roller). Start by marking the centerline of the chair seat from the front edge to the back. Center the first 1⅛-inch stripe over the centerline. Continue marking guidelines, working out from the center to each side. Plan for the middle set of guidelines to be the painted center stripe. Working out from the center, pencil an X in every other stripe to indicate that these stripes will not be painted.

4. Pour a small amount of glaze mixture onto a foam plate or into a paint tray. Evenly load stencil roller with white glaze mixture. Using a light touch and even pressure, roll stripes on chair seat following the guidelines (see photo A). If you make a mistake, use a wet paper towel to wipe off the area, let dry and roll again. Let dry. Erase any pencil marks.

5. Starting at the back of chair seat, use a pencil and quilters ruler to lightly mark guidelines 1⅛" apart for horizontal stripes. Make sure the lines run evenly across the chair and line up from edge to edge.

6. Paint the stripes as above to complete the gingham pattern (see photo B). Let dry. Erase any visible pencil marks and touch up with paint or glaze if necessary.

7. Seal with clear matte sealer to protect the finish.

8. For the tabletop, use the same process, this time starting with a white basecoat. Measure and mark with 1½" guidelines (the width of the trim roller) as above. Mix one part sky-blue paint with two parts glaze base (Test transparency of glaze on scrap board as above.) Use trim roller to apply both sets of stripes, as above, letting paint dry and erasing pencil marks in between applications. Let dry, then apply sealer.

SHOPPING LIST

- Table and chairs
- Flat latex paint in white and sky blue
- Scrap board
- Glaze base
- Quilters ruler
- Pencil
- Paper towels
- Foam plates or small paint tray
- 1⅛"-wide stencil roller (for chairs)
- 1½"-wide trim roller (for tabletop)
- White drafting eraser
- Clear matte sealer

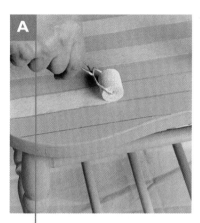

A

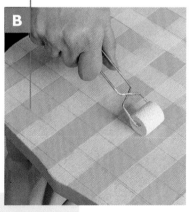

B

TAPE-AND-PAINT OPTION

FOR A MORE OPAQUE, UNIFORM LOOK, mask off the squares with painters tape and use flat paint in two values of the same shade, such as light and medium green, rather than overlapping layers of glaze. After base-coating with white or cream, mark a checkerboard grid on your furniture surface using a pencil and yardstick, selecting a square size proportionate to your piece. Using the pencil lines as a guide, tape off and paint sections of the grid in three separate steps. In every other horizontal row, tape off every other square and apply the darker color. Let dry and remove tape. Tape off and paint the remaining squares in those rows with lighter color. In the remaining horizontal rows, paint every other square with the lighter color. Let dry and remove tape to reveal the pattern.

LAYERED *Wash*

SHOPPING LIST

- Five-drawer dresser
- Flat latex paint in light tan, deep melon and rust
- Three paint trays
- 3" or 4" chip brushes
- White copy paper
- Painters tape
- Acrylic craft paint in black
- Artist brushes
- Pencil
- Transfer paper
- Paper towels
- Clear matte sealer
- Ten knobs in two different patterns

1. Prepare piece as needed, removing hardware and drawers to make painting easier.

2. In a paint tray, mix one part light tan paint with one part water, blending well. Apply this tan wash to the entire piece using a chip brush. Let paint dry.

3. Create two more washes as above, using deep melon paint for one and rust paint for the other.

4. For a two-tone look, apply alternating colorwashes in 1-foot sections. Start on one side of dresser and use a chip brush to apply deep melon wash to the first section. Let paint set 10 to 30 seconds, and then wipe away excess with a paper towel (see photo A). Vary paint application and soften section edges. Paint the next section using rust wash, blending the sections together and overlapping washes. Continue until the side is complete. Let dry. Apply another layer of rust wash to lightly frame the outer edges of the dresser side. Repeat the technique on rest of cabinet. Highlight the centers of the sides, top and front with additional layers of deep melon wash.

5. Plan color and pattern placement for the drawers. (We alternated base colors on the drawers, applying rust wash to the top, center and bottom drawer fronts and deep melon wash to the drawers in between. Three different designs decorate the rust-washed drawer fronts and freehand stripes add pattern to the melon-washed drawer fronts.)

6. Use a chip brush to apply the desired colorwash to each drawer front. If the application is too light, wait a few minutes and repeat. Apply the alternate colorwash to the beveled edges of each drawer. Let paint dry.

7. Make a paper pattern to fit each melon-washed drawer front using shapes from stencils, fabrics or other sources to create evenly spaced motifs, such as fleur-de-lis, scrolls or simple flowers.

8. Lay a piece of transfer paper on the drawer front with the appropriate pattern on top and tape in place. Trace pattern with pencil, pressing firmly to transfer designs (see photo B). Lift paper periodically to check transfer. Remove papers.

9. On rust-washed drawers, paint pattern details with deep melon wash. Highlight with a water-thinned blend of tan and deep melon paints (see photo C). Add shadow with water-thinned rust paint mixed with a touch of black acrylic paint.

10. Paint freehand striped designs on the melon-washed drawers using an artist brush and rust wash. Let dry.

11. Apply sealer. Add decorative knobs or drawer pulls.

HOT HARDWARE ....

ADD EVEN MORE PATTERN by replacing existing knobs or drawer pulls with a mix-and-match assortment, choosing shapes and materials that fit with the handpainted motifs and the style of your piece. On this dresser, we used two different styles of weathered copper knobs, highlighting the raised portions on the knobs with a touch of black acrylic paint to bring out the detailing.

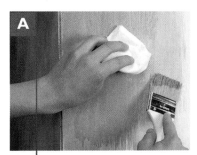

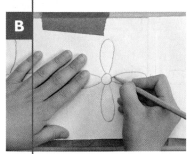

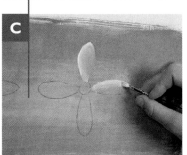

Screen-Print *Stencil*

1. Prepare piece for painting. Remove the doors and knobs. Lay doors flat. Paint the knobs, armoire doors and the shelves in the open shelving area with purple paint. Let dry.

2. Plan the stencil design layout on the doors. We stenciled only on the top doors. The full length of our stencil was too long for the doors, so we modified the design by omitting one circle of leaves and adding an extra dot at the bottom. This allows the stencil to be centered and spaced evenly from the top and bottom of the door panel.

3. After determining placement and spacing, use painters tape to secure the first stencil layer.

4. Cut a piece of screen the same size as the stencil. Use painters tape to secure the screen on top of the stencil. (Taping the screen in place prevents it from moving during stenciling.)

5. Apply white stencil cream to a stencil brush and begin at the top of the stencil, gently filling it in by pouncing the brush through the screen (see photo A). Add paint to the brush as needed for even application. Before removing the first stencil, line up the registration marks of the second stencil on top of the first. Carefully remove the first stencil.

6. Spray lightly with clear matte sealer for a temporary seal to protect the stencil.

7. Tape the second stencil in place. (Be careful not to smear the stencil cream when moving the stencil.) Tape the screen on top of the stencil. Proceed in the same manner with the remaining stencils by lining up the registration marks to align the pattern.

8. Pour white glaze on a foam plate. Using a foam brush, paint the indented trim around the door panels and the backs of the shelves of the open shelving area, going over the purple paint. Let dry.

9. When paint is completely dry, in about a week, brush clear matte sealer onto the door panels to protect the stenciled finish.

10. Reattach the knobs and the doors on the armoire.

A

JAZZED-UP STENCILS ....

ANOTHER WAY TO ADD A BURST OF PATTERN to stenciled motifs is to pair them with smaller allover stencils, such as dots, checks, diamonds or tiny florals. Start with a main stencil that has a fairly straightforward shape or motif. Look for a stencil sheet that is large enough to cover your main stencil or at least one complete section of your main stencil. Tape the allover stencil atop your main stencil as we did above with the screen.

SCANDINAVIAN *Florals*

1. After prepping the surface, paint cabinet and doors with several coats of white paint. Let each coat dry thoroughly and sand lightly with 400-grit sandpaper between coats. Wipe surface with a tack cloth before applying the next coat.

2. Apply several coats of sealer. (For this treatment, a sealer is needed for several reasons. It protects the base color while allowing you to wipe off mistakes easily, and it provides a smooth, slick surface for the tools to glide across without dragging.) Let dry. Mask off edges of door panels with painters tape.

3. Mix one part ocean blue paint with three parts glaze base. (Practice applying the glaze mixture and using the shaper tools on the shiny side of butcher paper cut to the size of the door panels before working on the cabinet.) Use a foam brush to smoothly apply the blue glaze mixture to the surface, brushing out any heavy deposits. Brush from one end of the surface to the other in a continuous stroke. To prevent heavy spots or unwanted lines, do not lift the brush until it is beyond the edge of the piece.

4. Use the cup round tool to make the flower stems, the comma strokes under the leaves, the small leaves under the flower heads and the flower centers. Use the 1½" flat tool to make the S-shaped leaves and flower petals (see photo A). Let dry. Refer to the tip box for more information on how to use the tools and correct mistakes.

5. Remove tape and clean up where needed with baby wipes. Use a cotton swab dipped in alcohol to lift off small spots of excess dried glaze.

6. Mask off the band that surrounds the panel with painters tape, then brush glaze mixture onto this area. Remove the tape and clean up as before. Let dry.

7. Protect panels with several coats of satin varnish.

SHOPPING LIST

- Entertainment cabinet
- Semigloss latex paint in white
- 400-grit sandpaper
- Tack cloth
- Clear matte sealer
- Painters tape
- Acrylic craft paint in ocean blue
- Glaze base
- Butcher paper with shiny coated surface
- Shaper tools in #10 cup round and 1½" firm flat
- 3" foam brushes
- Baby wipes
- Cotton swab
- Alcohol
- Satin interior varnish

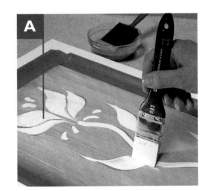

A

USING SHAPER TOOLS

GRIP THE SHAPER TOOL LIKE A CALLIGRAPHY PEN, with the head of the tool held constant at one angle so the line goes from thick to thin as the stroke curves. When you've gripped the tool correctly, drag it through the glaze to create the different strokes. Try to match general placement and size of strokes, but don't worry about making an exact match. You may need to redo the design several times until you are satisfied, but because you are pulling color off an evenly applied background, it is hard to redo just one area. Brush away previous work and start over before the glaze begins to dry. If the glaze has begun to set, wipe off what you can and use baby wipes to clean up the residue.

BEFORE

CREATIVE *Combing*

1. If necessary, cut pieces of plywood to replace your tabletops (ours were 10 inches by 16 inches, 12 inches by 18 inches and 14 inches by 20 inches.)

2. Apply primer to tabletops with a foam roller. Let dry.

3. Base-coat tabletops with pale gold paint. Let dry.

4. Lay tabletops flat on kraft paper. (Work on one tabletop at a time. If you want to alter the pattern design, you must do it while the glaze mixture is wet.)

5. Mix one part copper latex paint with three parts glaze in a paint tray.

6. Determine what pattern you would like for each tabletop. Patterns are created by the way you draw the comb through the glaze. We used moiré—a wavy pattern made by sets of parallel lines that overlap at opposing angles—on the largest tabletop, basketweave for the medium tabletop and zigzag for the smallest. To start all patterns, roll on a coat of copper glaze mixture. Create patterns as indicated below. (To prevent accidental smears, right-handed persons should begin work at the upper left corner; left-handed persons at the upper right.) As you complete each pattern section, wipe excess glaze on a paper towel.

7. For moiré, hold the comb at a 45-degree angle and drag it through the glaze in vertical wavy rows. Try to create close, evenly spaced rows. While the glaze is still wet, comb horizontal wavy rows, as above, across the vertical pattern (see photo A). Let dry.

8. To help create even squares for the basketweave pattern, mark guidelines on the kraft paper. Starting at one corner, mark every 3 inches around the sides of the tabletop. (Adjust measurements to fit your tabletop.) Starting at one of the top corners, comb down vertically to form a 3-inch square, following guidelines. Next to the first square, comb horizontally to make a second 3-inch square. Continue alternating vertical and horizontal squares across the top row (see photo B). Align the second row directly below the first and begin with a horizontally combed square. Continue across each row until the tabletop is complete, making sure all adjoining squares have alternate patterns. Let dry.

9. For the zigzag pattern, begin in an upper corner and drag the comb through the glaze, pulling down and sharply moving up repeatedly as you move horizontally across the tabletop. (Hold the tool firmly with a stiff wrist while moving your arm to create the pattern.) For the second row, begin the zigzag 1-inch below the first, leaving a solid section of glaze between rows (see photo C). (Adjust spacing to fit your tabletop.) Repeat until the tabletop is complete. Let dry.

10. Apply a coat of clear matte sealer to all tabletops and let dry. Install tabletops into the wrought-iron bases.

MAKE YOUR OWN COMBS

THOUGH YOU CAN PURCHASE VARIOUS STYLES and sizes of rubber or metal combs, you can also make your own from a rubber squeegee or a piece of cardboard. Choose a cardboard piece or squeegee that fits the area you wish to comb. Using a ruler and pen, measure and mark equally spaced teeth of the same size along the edge of the cardboard or squeegee and cut out with a sharp craft knife.

SHOPPING LIST

- Set of stacking tables with wrought-iron bases
- ½" plywood for replacement tabletops (optional)
- White latex primer
- Ruler
- Three 4" foam paint rollers
- Three paint trays
- Flat latex paint in pale gold and copper
- Glaze base
- Kraft paper
- Combing tool
- Paper towels
- Clear matte sealer

A

B

C

BEFORE

MAD FOR *Plaid*

ADD PUNCH TO A BEDROOM with a plaid lingerie chest. Base-coat the chest with cream-colored paint. Plan your plaid design on paper with colored pencils to experiment with colors and stripe widths. When you're ready to start working on your piece, use various widths of painters tape as a spacing guide rather than measuring and marking every stripe. Simply tape the whole surface and remove tape from areas as you paint them. Here, we used 1" and 2" tape for the larger stripes and ½" tape for the narrow stripes. Mix terra-cotta, green and gold glazes, using two parts glaze and one part paint for each. Tape off all horizontal stripes on one side of your piece. Complete one color at a time, using a foam brush that matches the stripe width. Remove tape and let the first color dry before moving to the next. Repeat for other colors, adding or removing tape as needed. For the narrower stripes, apply three rows of tape side by side centered over desired areas. Remove the middle row of tape and apply paint. Remove tape and let dry before beginning the entire process again with vertical rows of stripes to create the plaid pattern (see photo).

Complete each section of the piece, including each drawer front, separately for consistency. If your piece has beveled edges, like the drawers on this chest, tape them off and paint with a solid color. Use another solid color for the knobs, if desired.

CONNECT THE DOTS

LIVEN UP A STAID CABINET with perky polka dots. Begin with a white base coat. Once that's dry, plan your dot pattern, choosing a size of dot and spacing that best fits your piece. To ensure even spacing, create a temporary grid pattern to follow using an art projector. Draw a grid onto a transparency and project it onto your piece. Dip the round tip of a small foam paint roller into pale green paint and press it against the piece at the grid intersections to make the dots. You can make several dots before reloading the roller tip with paint.

BEFORE

FRENCH TWIST

CREATE A DRAMATIC STAMPED EFFECT by teaming two high-contrast colors, such as white and a warm, midtone hue (we used terra-cotta.) The contrast enables even small-scale motifs, like this fleur-de-lis, to make a big impression. Paint your piece a rich midtone hue. When the base coat is dry, determine size, orientation and placement of stamps to best fit your piece. For interest, alternate the direction of your stamped images. Mark placement lightly with pencil. Next, apply a thin, even coat of white paint to the back of the center stamp in your design and press it firmly in place. Work from the center stamp outward to complete your stamped pattern. Carry the look throughout your room by using the same technique on a different piece in a reverse color combination.

ABOREAL *Armoire*

PAIR STENCILING WITH A NEGATIVE FAUX FINISH to lend depth and character to a large-scale furniture piece. Here, a mottled tone-on-tone green glaze is a verdant backdrop for a leafy stencil. Begin with a base coat of white paint or primer. Mix a medium lime glaze and a light olive glaze. The glaze should be thin enough to manipulate and lighter than the stencil color. Working on one section of the piece at a time, apply the lime glaze and pull it up immediately with a large piece of plastic drop cloth. The wrinkles in the plastic produce a textured look. Continue the technique to complete the entire piece, using fresh plastic on each section. When the first layer is dry, apply the olive glaze in the same manner. Plan stencil placement, then position stencil in place using spray adhesive. Pounce paint over stencil using a foam brush or makeup sponge, applying paint more heavily around the edges. Remove the stencil and, while the paint is still wet, use a damp sponge or cloth to lift off some paint from the middle of the patterns to create a timeworn effect. Continue stenciling, making sure to align pattern repeats.

PEEKABOO
Lace

CREATE DELICATE LACE PATTERNS ON FURNITURE in next to no time by using lace fabric as a stencil. Base-coat your piece with paint in a vanilla hue. When the paint is dry, measure the areas where you wish to add the lace effect and cut pieces of lace fabric to fit each area. To create mirror image on adjacent doors or panels, you can use the lace on one side, then flop it to use on the other. Secure the lace in place with painters tape, making sure it is wrinkle-free, and tape off all other areas you don't wish to paint. Apply a light gray spray paint (we used primer) over the lace, using a light, sweeping motion (see photo). Go over some areas more than others to add depth to the treatment, but don't spray too heavily in any one area or you may obscure the pattern. Before removing the lace, lift up a corner to make sure you are satisfied with the effect. If not, respray where needed. Remove the lace and tape to reveal the finished design.

PACKED WITH STYLE

WHO'D HAVE THOUGHT SHIPPING MATERIALS could be fodder for a fun printed treatment? Here, packing peanuts act as a stamp to add figure-eight patterns to a tabletop. Base-coat your piece as desired (we used crisp white). Pencil guidelines indicating where you plan to stamp (we stamped an outer and inner border that follows the shape of our tabletop). Select several packing peanuts of similar size and shape. (Avoid those made from organic materials such as cornstarch; they will begin to dissolve when they come into contact with the water in latex paint.) Pour a contrasting-color paint onto a foam plate and dip the edge of a peanut into the paint. Stamp the image onto your piece. Repeat the process, evenly spacing the imprints along the guidelines. Switch to a new peanut after a few uses or when it begins to lose its shape.

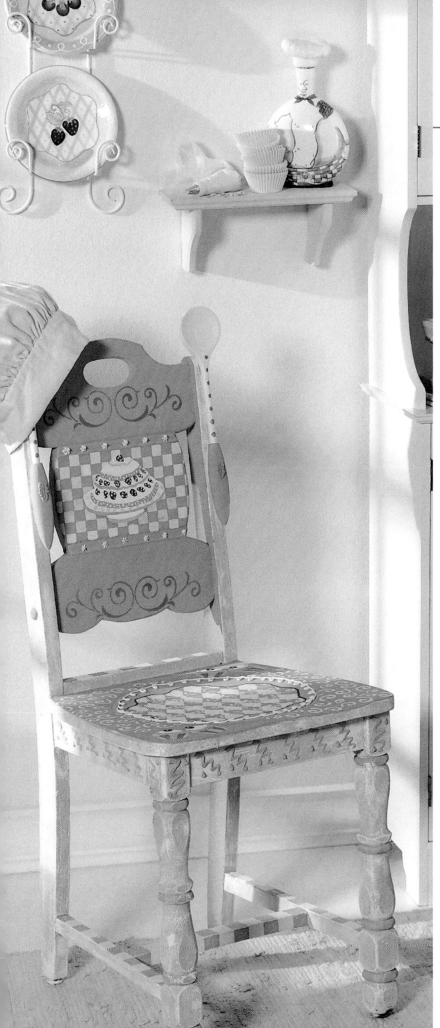

SWEET *Seat*

USE PASTEL ACRYLIC AND LATEX PAINTS with stencils and frosting-like modeling paste to sweeten up a plain chair with a bakery case full of pattern. Start by base-coating the legs and back uprights with lime paint. Dry brush white paint over the green for a powdered-sugar effect. Next, paint the seat top, chair back and stretcher bars with rose paint. Tape off stripes on stretcher bars and paint them yellow. Next, trace a large circle on the seat and draw a wavy line about 1 inch in from the edge. Paint the wavy border lime and define the inside edge with red paint. Use yellow paint and a stencil to create a harlequin design in the circle center. Use more stencils to add tiny flowers atop the harlequin pattern, swirls to the seat and scroll shapes and a checkerboard pattern to the seat back. Leave space on the chair seat to add handpainted or stenciled cupcakes at one front and one back corner. Also paint a pretty cake atop the checkerboard on the seat back using a stencil or your own imagination. To add dimension, paint wooden mixing spoons to match and hot glue them to the tops of the back uprights. For a finishing touch, apply modeling paste using a cake decorating bag and a variety of tips to add more pattern and dimension to various parts of the chair. You can tint the paste by kneading in a bit of paint. (This chair is best for decorative purposes; constant use may wear away the modeling paste.)

BEFORE

MIX & Match

30

34

36

WELL-DECORATED ROOM

needn't be filled with a suite of matching furniture. In fact, mixing and matching is becoming more popular as people realize that it boosts the character of interiors. However, you don't want to assemble a ragtag bunch of furnishings that seem at odds with one another because of incompatible styles or finishes. Here's where the power of paint comes in handy—you can use similar paint treatments and colors or repeating motifs to unite an odd lot with a consistent sense of style, be it rustic Scandinavian or French country flair.

RAMBLING *Roses*

BEFORE

1. Prepare pieces for painting.

2. Prime all pieces and let dry. Base-coat pieces with light tan paint. Let dry.

3. Create a wash by mixing one part deep rose paint to one part water. Do the same with the deep coral paint.

4. Apply wash with a paintbrush, using the same color for an entire piece or different colors on different sections of the same piece. (We used deep rose on well as the dresser top and frame and deep coral on the entire headboard and the drawers and side panels of the dresser.) Wipe off excess wash with a rag, removing more in raised areas.

5. Lay drawers flat. Brush wash horizontally across the front. If desired, use a rag to lightly wipe off excess wash at drawer centers for a translucent effect. Add wash to any parts that seem too pale. Let dry.

6. For the side panels of some of the pieces, use the technique in the Dreamy Drip Treatment (see box). Allow some of the wash to drip down the sides, creating a streaked effect. Let dry.

7. By tracing (and enlarging, if needed) motifs from gift wrap, wallpaper or another source, create flower patterns to fit drawers and other areas where you want to add flowers. (On our dresser, painted floral patterns continue from one drawer to the next.) Tape transfer paper onto furniture in desired location. Place the pattern on top of the transfer paper and trace pattern lines with a pencil.

8. Use both latex and acrylic paints for the floral and leaf details or create new colors. Thin paints, using a ratio of one part water to one part paint. Adjust the ratio to make darker or lighter colors, if desired.

9. Paint stems and leaves. With a liner brush, paint the leaf outline, then follow with a clean, wet round brush, pulling the paint from the outline into the center to create a central highlight and outer shadow. Apply paint lightly, adding more layers, if desired. If the first color is too pale, paint over it with another wash of color. When painting vines or long stems, pull liner brush smoothly, following the length of the vine. If you make a mistake, with a damp cloth and begin again.

10. As above, paint flower outlines with watered-down paint; then use a clean, wet artist brush to pull paint into the petal centers (see photo). Or, paint the whole flower, then wipe away paint from the center or add a lighter paint color to the center.

11. Apply sealer to protect finish.

GOLDEN *Oldies*

1. Find furniture pieces that will work together. Prepare surfaces for painting according to the finish type, applying stain-blocking primer, if needed.

2. Paint all pieces with two coats of golden yellow paint. Let dry.

3. With a hand sander and 100-grit sandpaper, sand along the edges of furniture where normal wear would occur. Use 220-grit paper to sand the detail areas. Sand to the point where the bare wood shows through to produce a distressed look (see photo A).

4. Highlight carved details with a contrasting color of paint, such as blue. Let dry. If you are attaching wood on accents, paint them and attach to the furniture with wood glue or brads. Using white paint, lightly dry brush over the blue details. Let dry.

5. Apply mocha glaze to furniture pieces. This antiquing technique is used to add instant patina and warmth to the surface; the brown glaze will collect in the crevices to highlight details and add to the distressed look. To create a consistent finish, work on a small section of one furniture piece—such as a chair seat—at a time, using a paintbrush to apply an even coat of glaze. Use a crumpled rag to pick up the glaze, turning the rag in different directions as you work to create a random design while removing excess glaze (see photo B). (To soften edges or hard lines between sections, add more glaze and blend with a rag.) Move to the next section, apply more glaze and rag off as above. Continue until the entire piece has been covered, working in small sections. Let dry for three to seven days.

6. For a weathered look, lightly sand the pieces using 220-grit sandpaper, then wipe with a tack cloth.

7. Embellish pieces with handpainted details, where desired. For example, paint a single rose on the center of a chair back and stamp a vine of leaves around the edge of the seat. For roses, first make a pencil dot on furniture to indicate flower center placement. Dip a 1" foam brush into straw-colored paint. Center the brush upright over the pencil mark and press against the surface, spinning it to create a circular shape. Let dry. Dip the tip of an artist brush into white acrylic paint and create three comma-shaped accent marks around the center of each rose. Let dry. Dip the wooden end of an artist brush in blue acrylic paint and place three dots at the center of each rose. Let dry. Use a small leaf stamp and light leaf green paint to stamp around the seat edge. Let dry.

8. Apply sealer to all pieces.

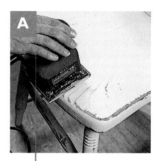

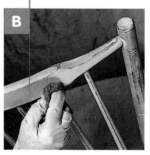

BEFORE

MATCH MAKING

USE MISMATCHED FURNITURE together in one room if the pieces are similar in style and line or have design elements that tie them together. On each one of our pieces, there were either raised or carved details. If your furniture does not have any such details and you like this look, add wooden accents purchased at a hardware store.

NATURALLY *Nordic*

HANDSOME HUTCH

1. Prepare surface for painting according to finish type, applying stain-blocking primer, if needed.

2. Base-coat hutch exterior with cream paint using a foam roller.

3. Tape off any areas that will not be aqua and base-coat the hutch interior with aqua using a foam roller.

4. To highlight hutch details such as beveled edges and arched details, accent them with aqua. Protect previously painted areas with painters tape.

5. Add floral details to glass doors and panels on hutch base (see Flower-Painting Technique for glass and wood surfaces, page 37).

6. Apply two coats of clear sealer. Add new glass drawer and door pulls.

7. Measure the length and depth of your piece, and create a paper cornice pattern for the back and sides of the hutch top. Look through furniture catalogs and magazines for shape ideas. Enlarge it to actual size, taping together photocopies, if needed.

8. Transfer patterns to 1 x 6 poplar board. Tape patterns to the board and slide transfer paper facedown between the board surface and patterns. Trace over pattern lines with pencil.

9. Use a jigsaw to cut out the cornice back and the two side pieces. Cut slowly along curved guidelines. Smooth rough edges with a wood file and then sand, progressing to finer grade sandpaper.

10. Butt side pieces against the front of the back piece at the corners. Predrill pilot holes through the cornice back into the edges of the side pieces and secure with wood screws.

11. Secure the cornice to the hutch top using flat mending plates on the back (see photo A) or predrill corresponding holes through the cornice's bottom edge and into the hutch top and secure with wood dowels and glue.

12. To soften contemporary lines, copy curved or other decorative details from your hutch. (Arched panels on our hutch's base inspired us to add curved inserts to every other glass door panel.)

13. Using tracing paper, copy design elements or other details. Enlarge or reduce the design to fit within the frame of the cabinet door using a photocopier. Use a right angle to make sure corners are square. To make sure insert will fit, cut a paper template and try it on the door.

14. Copy the final design onto hardboard. Lay transfer paper facedown on hardboard, and then place design pattern on top. Trace design with pencil to transfer.

15. Cut out inserts with a jigsaw. Sand edges smooth. Prime surfaces and paint both sides cream. Avoid getting paint on inset edges, as it will affect fit. Check fit by placing in cabinet door.

16. Install inserts to top of hutch door frame using wood glue (see photo B). Let dry.

17. Use wood putty to fill any gaps. Sand lightly, and then touch up with paint.

BEFORE

NATURALLY *Nordic*

Continued...

WOOD-GRAIN TABLE

1. Prepare surface for painting.

2. Base-coat table with seafoam green. Let dry.

3. Mix one part glaze base with one part aqua paint.

4. To mimic the look of edge-glued pine, use a 3"-wide chip brush, as it is the same width as the graining tool and will allow you to texturize paint in one stroke. Align one edge of the brush with the edge of the table, and pull the width of the brush down the length of the tabletop. The glaze should be applied fairly heavily; you will need enough to draw the graining tool through so that the pattern is noticeable.

5. To prevent the buildup of glaze, hold the graining tool slightly beyond table's edge in line with glazed strip. Then, pull the tool smoothly into the glaze and continue in one long stroke, gently rocking the tool as you go (see photo A). If you stop or hesitate midstroke, horizontal glaze lines will build up, creating an unnatural effect.

6. If you do not like the wood grain pattern, brush over the strip and pull the tool through the glaze again. If glaze starts to dry out, add more glaze or carefully use a wet wipe to remove the glaze down to the base coat and start again.

7. When satisfied, start the next strip as above, applying the glaze, and then rocking the tool through it in a slightly different way to vary the look of the grain. Move the tool parallel to the previous strip, making sure the edge of the tool just touches that strip. Repeat the process until the tabletop is complete.

8. For the curved areas or turned table legs, use a triangular or graduated combing tool to create grain lines. (These tools can bend to fit curves and different shapes.) Make sure there are no gaps between each combed strip, and always pull parallel to the previous strokes. Let dry.

9. Apply clear sealer to protect finish.

10. To soften finish and make it look aged, we used glaze to whitewash over the grain surface. Mix one part cream paint with one part glaze. Brush the glaze over a small section of the surface, and then wipe some away with a paper towel or rag, leaving some cream glaze trapped against the wood grain to highlight it. Work quickly to ensure areas blend together. If the grain color does not show enough, mist with water and wipe lightly. If needed, mist the surface before applying the glaze to keep it from drying too quickly. Let dry and seal.

11. Add floral details (see Flower-Painting Technique for wood surfaces, page 37). When dry, seal piece.

(see Flower-Painting Technique for wood surfaces, page 37)

SHOPPING LIST

- Table
- Stain-blocking primer
- Flat latex paint in seafoam green, aqua and cream
- Glaze base
- 3" chip brushes
- Rocker-style wood-graining tool
- Triangular or graduated combing tools
- Clear matte sealer
- Water-filled spray bottle
- Paper towels
- Baby wipes

A

For wood and glass surfaces, create a floral pattern by copying a motif from gift wrap, wallpaper, a stencil or another source, adapting it to fit your piece. You may need to make several photocopies and tape them together to fill the space.

WOOD SURFACES

Set the pattern in place where desired, and slide a piece of transfer paper facedown beneath it. Trace over the pattern lines with a pencil to transfer the design. Use an artist brush and teal acrylic paint to paint the stem and tendrils, and then outline the flower and portions of the leaves (see photo). Thin paint slightly with water for a more transparent look. When painting narrow lines, dip the brush in water before picking up paint to create a smooth brush stroke. Use raw sienna paint to create shadows next to the teal outline on flowers and leaves. Paint a shadow around flower center. Use cream paint to lightly fill in the petals and leaves. Lightly pat glaze base over the flower and blot off with a damp cloth.

GLASS SURFACES

For glass pieces, paint on the inside of the glass for a cleaner look and to protect the finish. Clean the glass surface and prepare for glass paint following the manufacturer's instructions. You may need to apply a conditioner that allows the paint to bond to the glass. On the outside of the glass panel, tape pattern copies facedown. Using an artist brush, paint stems and tendrils with brown glass paint and then outline one half of each flower petal, leaf and details with the same color (see photo). As you work, lift the pattern paper to see the paint. If you do not like the effect, remove or add colors. You can combine glass paint thinner or glaze with the paint to create a smoother line. Outline the entire flower petal and leaf along the inside of the brown paint lines using taupe glass paint. Dip a small sea sponge in ivory glass paint and lightly dab to fill in leaves and flower centers. Let dry. Repeat for other glass panels. Using a foam brush, seal and protect just the painted design with the appropriate sealer.

AIR CHAIR

FRESHEN UP A WOOD DINING CHAIR by using a white-wash applied with a dry brush. To begin, prepare the surface. To make whitewash, mix one part glaze with one part cream paint. Dip the tip of a chip brush into the glaze mixture, and then tap it on a paper towel to remove excess paint and separate bristles. The dry brush strokes will mimic the look of wood grain. Work on one part of the chair at a time. Paint with long strokes, and follow the direction of the chair's wood grain to create the look of faux wood grain (see photo). Complete the stroke from one edge to the other without lifting the brush. Apply brush strokes side by side until the entire piece is painted. Transfer flower design to chair's backsplat, and paint it following the Flower-Painting Technique for wood surfaces (at right).

STAINS
&Dyes

COLORED STAINS AND DYES add vibrant

color to bare wood. Unlike paint, which sits on top of

the surface, stains and dyes penetrate the wood fiber.

Combined with the natural wood tones, they create a

transparent layered effect that enhances the beauty of

the grain. In addition to standard wood stains, you can

also use sheer floral sprays and fabric dyes to color

wood. Use colors as is or custom blend them for unique

hues. And you don't have to stick to stain alone—pair

it with oil pencils to create patterns in resist or add a

bit of stenciling to embellish a stained surface.

BUILD A CABINET

WE MADE OUR CABINET using eight unfinished two-drawer CD boxes. We placed two stacks of four boxes side by side, attached them together with construction adhesive and secured them with screws to a base made from a cabinet door panel. To finish the piece, we added bun feet to the bottom of the panel. We stained the cabinet exterior red and the feet green. The drawers alternate between blue and green, each in three graduated shades created with layers of stain and masking tape.

GRADUATED-SQUARES *Cabinet*

SHOPPING LIST

- Unfinished cabinet
- Various grades of sandpaper
- Tack cloth
- Metal straightedge
- Drill and drill bit
- Spray stain in leaf green, denim blue and apple red
- Rags or paper towels
- 1" painters tape
- Craft knife
- Clear spray sealer
- Brushed aluminum knobs

1. Remove drawers and lightly sand all areas of cabinet that will be stained with 120-grit sandpaper. (If your piece has knobs, remove these as well).

2. If your piece doesn't have knobs, mark knob placement on the center of each drawer front. Predrill holes to fit knob hardware at marked points.

3. Divide drawers into two even groups, one for each color. Apply a base coat of either blue or green stain to the drawer fronts. Spray stain on the wood, let set 30 seconds, then wipe off to spread the color evenly over the surface (see photo A). If the surface color is uneven, re-spray to dissolve the first layer and wipe immediately. (This coat seals the bare wood.) Spray about ¼ inch over the drawer edges so unstained areas are not noticeable when the drawer is placed in the cabinet.

4. Spray the cabinet exterior with apple red, applying stain and wiping off as above. (Do not try to achieve a deep color in one application; build up light layers, gradually deepening the color.)

5. To create graduated squares on the blue drawers, which move outward from light to dark, apply concentric rows of 1" tape to the entire drawer front, then remove one row at a time between applications of stain, using the width of the tape as a mask. Start at the outside edge of a drawer front, applying a row of tape around the perimeter. Place a second row of tape inside the first (see photo B). (You can overlap the tape at the corner; it will be cut away in the next step.) Fill in the center with a few rows of tape placed side by side until the area is covered. Tape all blue drawer fronts.

6. Align a metal straightedge with the inside edge of the outermost row of tape and use a craft knife to cut through any overlapping tape. This frees the second row of tape so it will leave a border when removed. Cut around the edge of the center square as above, using the inside edge of the second row of tape as a guide. Repeat on all blue drawer fronts.

7. Lift off the outer row of tape. Press down the edges of the remaining taped areas. Evenly spray the drawer fronts with a second layer of blue stain. Apply a light, uniform coat. Do not wipe away the stain. Let dry. (You will be applying another layer of color in the next step. Do not overspray, which may cause the stain to blob or run.) As you wait for coats to dry, work on other portions of the cabinet.

8. Lift the second row of tape from, leaving the center square covered. Press down the edges of the center square. Spray as above and let dry. (If you want greater contrast, re-tape the second row and apply another layer of stain to the outer row.) Carefully remove the center square immediately after you spray, using the tip of the craft knife to lift a corner (see photo C). If any stain seeps under the loose tape, let dry thoroughly, then use a craft knife to carefully scrape away irregular areas.

9. On the green drawers, we applied rows of tape after each layer of stain. The dark-to-light pattern moves from the center outward; the color of the outermost row is the base-coat color. Apply a row of 1" tape to the green drawer fronts following the perimeter. Press the edges down to prevent the stain from seeping underneath. Spray drawers with a second coat of stain, applying the color as above. Let dry.

10. Apply the second row of tape, following the inner edge of the first row. Press the edges of the tape down and spray a third layer of stain to create the center square. Remove tape and let dry thoroughly. Repeat for all green drawers.

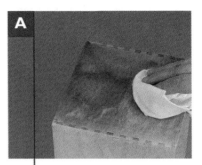

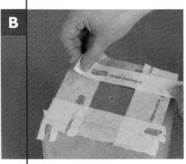

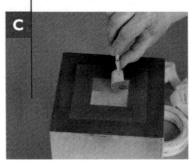

11. Apply several coats of clear sealer. Let each coat dry and sand lightly, following the grain, between applications. Wipe with a tack cloth before spraying again.

12. Add decorative knobs to the front of each drawer and replace drawers in cabinet, alternating colors.

BUTTERFLY
Garden

1. Plan your design and placement of motifs on your furniture piece. (We created a continuous design down the front of our chest and placed single motifs on the sides and top of the chest as accents.) When creating your design, look for easily transferable outlines and images in clip-art books or software, on wallpaper or fabric and in coloring or children's books. Use simple stencils or trace figural templates to create some of your motifs. Sketch, trace or stencil your motifs on pieces of paper sized to fit the top, drawer fronts and sides of your furniture piece.

2. Tape patterns to drawer fronts, making sure design is aligned down the front of piece. Tape patterns to sides of chest and top of chest where desired.

3. Slide a piece of transfer paper facedown between each pattern and wood surface. Trace over each pattern to transfer designs.

4. Begin to fill in the pattern using colored oil pencils. If you included vines that climb from one drawer to the next, outline the vines and draw in the veins of the leaves with dark green. Color the remainder of the leaves with bright green.

5. Color the motifs using bright colors and add texture to some of the designs by letting some of the wood show through. Color some lighter-hued areas very solidly to make sure they show up after the dye application.

6. Create a textural and shaded background on the entire chest by overlapping groups of short, parallel pencil strokes in different directions (see photo A). Start with yellow and light green pencils at the top of the chest,

working into deeper shades of green as you move down the front and ending with touches of blue on the bottom.

7. Mix dyes in separate containers using warm water. (It is not necessary to add the salt mentioned in the manufacturer's instructions since this is not fabric.) Let dyes cool slightly before application.

8. Using a chip brush, apply the dye sparingly to chosen motifs (we brushed our leaves with Burgundy) and build up the color (see photo B). Stay within the colored lines to prevent the dye from spreading. (Test dye on scrap wood before you apply it to the piece; you can't reverse the process.)

9. Apply a coat of dye over the entire piece (we used Sunflower), starting at the top. While this is still wet, apply a slightly watered-down third color of dye (we used Vivid Turquoise), starting at the bottom of the chest and quickly working up the bottom third of the cabinet. Accent the vines, leaves or other desired motifs by lightly brushing the third dye around them (see photo C).

10. Let dry several days. Coat with sealer. The finish will heighten the color. (As the dye dries, the color may fade. Avoid placing the piece in direct sunlight.)

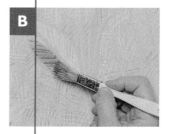

USING OIL PENCILS AND DYE

THE MORE SOLIDLY YOU FILL in an area with oil pencil, the brighter the color will appear. Leaving spaces where some wood shows through can make a color look different after the dye application. For example, we colored the leaves bright green, using small lines to fill in the centers. After dyes were applied, the leaves appeared to have an olive cast when viewed from a distance.

CAPTIVATING *Copper*

SHOPPING LIST

- Unfinished pine buffet
- Clean cotton rags
- Water-based wood stain in deep green
- Background stencil with allover scrolled design
- Stencil adhesive spray
- Painters tape
- Acrylic craft paint in metallic copper
- Wedge-shaped makeup sponges
- 1" foam brush
- Paper towel
- Clear matte sealer
- Copper knobs (optional)

1. Select a furniture piece with an unfinished wood surface and prepare for staining.

2. Choose a stain color that coordinates with your stencil paint. (Test the selected stain on a hidden area of the piece to determine whether you like the color.)

3. Apply the stain with a clean cotton rag, following the direction of the wood grain (see photo A). Allow the stain to penetrate, but while the stain is still wet, wipe away excess, following the grain. Stain or paint door pulls or purchase copper-finished hardware. Let the stain dry for 2 hours. (To increase the color intensity, apply a second coat of stain.)

4. Select a stencil with an allover design. To cover an area larger than the stencil, move the stencil and align the design repeat as needed. (We chose a single-layer 8-inch by 11-inch stencil with an overall scrolled design to apply to the drawer front and two door panels of our buffet.)

5. Apply spray adhesive to the stencil back and let dry until tacky.

6. Mask drawer edges and cabinet door panels using painters tape. Position the stencil near one end of the drawer front and work from this end toward the other to ensure proper design matching. Lightly dab a makeup sponge into copper metallic paint. Blot excess paint on a paper towel. With a pouncing motion, apply paint to the stencil, starting at the outside edges of the design and working inward (see photo B). Remove stencil and let dry.

7. Move the stencil to the next section on the drawer, align the pattern and continue stenciling to cover the entire surface. Repeat on the door panels. Let dry.

8. Before painting decorative edges and recessed areas on doors and drawer fronts, protect surrounding areas with painters tape. Dip a 1" foam brush into copper paint and apply to the masked-off areas. Let dry.

9. Apply sealer to the entire cabinet to protect finish.

10. Finish the existing knobs to match or attach new copper knobs to coordinate.

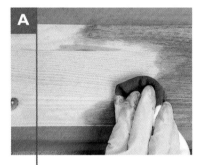

STENCILING OVER STAIN

TO ADD AN ELEGANT GLEAM to this pine buffet, we stenciled light-catching copper metallic accents atop a deep green stain. Though metallics look especially sophisticated atop a deep color (think gold with cranberry or silver with black), you can also try other paint/stain combinations. For example, stencil in pale blue atop a white stain for a light, Swedish-style look or try pink stenciling with a pale green stained backdrop for garden appeal.

STRIPE IT *Rich*

SHOPPING LIST

- Unfinished round butcher-block table with traditional pedestal base
- Water-based wood conditioner
- Straightedge
- Craft knife
- Foam paintbrushes
- Water-based wood stain in white, light yellow, cinnamon, light green and golden oak
- Soft, clean rags
- Clear semigloss sealer
- Painters tape

1. Prepare the surface for staining.

2. Using a foam brush, apply an even coat of wood conditioner to the entire piece, following manufacturer's instructions.

3. Determine pattern. We used the strips of hardwood on the butcher-block tabletop as the basis for our striped pattern. Do not begin or end the pattern in the middle of a wood strip; instead use the edges of the widths of wood strips as pattern lines. For our pattern, we created a white center area of approximately six strips. On either side of the center area, we stained two strips in cinnamon. Next to the cinnamon is one strip of light green, then three strips of light yellow. We then applied white to the remainder of the tabletop on either side of the striped pattern. (The size of the strips may vary, depending on the tabletop, even among the same-size tabletop from the same manufacturer. Adapt the design for the size of strips on your particular table. Use the butcher-block strips of your table to determine the exact width of your pattern stripes.)

4. With a straightedge and craft knife, score the top side of the tabletop in the pattern you have determined, using the strips of the butcher block as a guide. Score the edge of the tabletop as well. The scoring should be approximately 2 to 3 millimeters deep, just enough to feel when you run your hand across the table. The scoring helps prevent the stain from seeping beyond the determined area.

5. Prior to applying stain to the tabletop, stain a test patch on the underside or on a piece of scrap wood to determine how quickly the wood absorbs the stain. For a transparent look, wipe off the stain within 30 seconds or less; the more time that passes, the more opaque the stain will become.

6. Tape off the scored lines that determine the edges of the stripe to be stained for added protection against seepage. Once tape is in place, press down firmly in order to ensure proper adhesion.

7. Apply the stain. (We applied the stain differently than recommended by the manufacturer, using a foam brush in quick, sweeping motions. When applying stain in this manner, do not soak the wood; this increases the chance of seepage. The brush should not be too dry, however, or the finish will appear uneven.) Start with the lightest color, white, and apply stain with foam brush in quick, sweeping motions, following the wood grain. Wipe with a cloth immediately, following the grain. Continue for all white areas, including the edge of the table. (We applied two coats of white to the center area of the striped pattern and one coat to the remainder of the tabletop outside of the striped pattern.) Remove tape immediately after staining and wipe up any seepage. Let dry thoroughly before staining the adjacent color stripe.

8. Repeat staining process for remaining colors, applying one coat of each (see photo A) and allowing each to dry thoroughly in between. Stain the table base with golden oak, following manufacturer's instructions. Let dry overnight.

9. Apply sealer, following manufacturer's instructions. (Be sure to seal the entire table to prevent warping. We recommend applying two to three coats, sanding between coats. Assemble table according to manufacturer's instructions.)

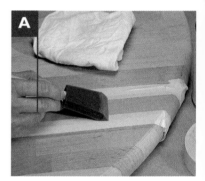

TIP: *When staining, build up layers of color. Start off with a transparent application and add another coat if a richer color is desired. It is always easier to add rather than subtract color when staining.*

MIXING DYE

FOR LIQUID DYE, shake the bottle thoroughly, then mix 1 tablespoon dye to 1 cup hot water. For powdered dye, mix 1 teaspoon dye to 1 cup hot water, stirring thoroughly to activate dye. Though this is a cold-water fabric dye, hot water is needed to activate the color. The hotter the water, the more vibrant the color. If the dye cools during use, reheat it gently in a microwave or on a stove top. Experiment with the water-to-dye ratio to find the right color depth. The consistency of the dye should allow the wood grain to show through. If the dye is too opaque, it will look like paint rather than stain.

COLOR-BLOCK *Mirror*

1. Arrange wooden blocks on the frame until you are pleased with the design. (We used a pattern of 16 blocks down the length of the mirror frame on one side, reversing the order on the opposite side. We used two blocks to fill the top and bottom sides of the frame, again reversing the order.)

2. Select dye colors. (We used nine dye mixtures—eight colors for the blocks and one for the frame.) Use some straight from the package and custom-mix others (see box, below).

3. Determine the order in which the colors will be applied to the wooden blocks. (We used eight colors in a sequence, repeating yellow twice. Using 36 blocks, the color pattern worked out evenly.) Adjust the number of colors in your pattern sequence to work out evenly for your number of blocks. Ensure proper block placement by numbering them and indicating the dye color on the back of each block.

4. Sand the surface of each block and the mirror frame, wiping all pieces with a tack cloth to remove any dust.

5. Mix the dyes (see box at left). (Wear rubber gloves and cover your work area with newspapers and a plastic drop cloth for protection.)

6. Use a paintbrush to apply dye to the blocks, using the markings on the backs of the blocks as your guide. (Because the dye works better when it is hot (see box), only use one color at a time, staining all blocks of that color before mixing and using a new color. Dip paintbrush into hot dye mixture and spread evenly until wood is saturated (see photo A). (This technique is similar to watercolor painting; the dye will be very liquid and may drip.) Let dry approximately 5 minutes, then wipe off excess dye with a cloth. Repeat the process until you are satisfied with the depth of the color. Let dry completely. Continue in this manner for the remaining colors and blocks, staining the mirror frame as well. Allow all pieces to air dry.

7. When pieces are completely dry, lightly sand and remove excess dust with a tack cloth.

8. Protect blocks with satin-finish sealer. Let dry.

9. Determine and mark the exact placement of the each block so they are evenly spaced along the frame. We allowed approximately ½ inch between each block.

10. Apply construction adhesive to the back of a block (see photo B), then place it in the predetermined location, pressing firmly to adhere. Wipe away any excess glue with a damp cloth. Repeat process to adhere all blocks to frame.

SHOPPING LIST

- 36 wooden plinth blocks in varying rosette and bull's-eye patterns
- Full-length mirror with wood frame wide enough for blocks
- Sandpaper
- Tack cloth
- Cold-water dye in various bright colors
- Rubber gloves
- Plastic containers with lids (for dye)
- Paintbrush
- Clear satin sealer
- Ruler
- Construction adhesive
- Plastic drop cloth and newspaper

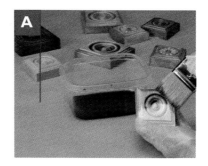

A

CUSTOM-MIXING COLORS

COLD-WATER DYE colors can be mixed to create a variety of shades. For example, you can mix one part seafoam green and one part yellow to get turquoise or two parts purple and one part royal blue to get deep purple. Experiment to create your own hues.

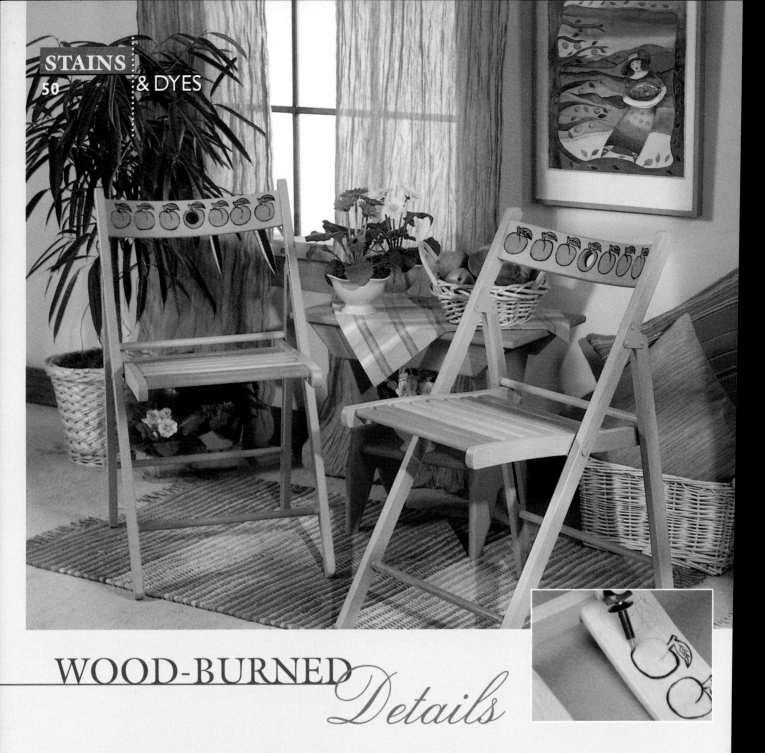

WOOD-BURNED *Details*

SELECT AN UNFINISHED FURNITURE PIECE and prepare the surface for staining. Choose a design for your piece. We applied row of seven evenly spaced peaches across the back of wood folding chairs then repeated the bright stain colors on the rest of the chair. Draw or trace a simple design, like a fruit or a flower, adapting it to fit your piece. Use transfer paper to transfer the motifs to desired locations on your piece. Pencil in details, such as leaf veins and peach cleft. Repeat motif as desired, spacing evenly. Place the universal point on a wood-burning tool. Gripping the tool like a pencil, use light pressure to pull the tool along the pencil lines, outlining the motif and its details (see photo). The longer the point remains on the wood surface, the darker and deeper the wood burning will be. For each stain color, combine one part acrylic paint with one part staining medium. Apply stain inside the wood-burned motifs using a foam brush. Wipe off excess stain with a clean rag. Reapply stain until you achieve the desired shade. Brush desired color stain onto the furniture surface around the motifs. Wipe off excess with clean cloth until you achieve the desired shade. Repeat, if necessary. Use a cotton swab to reach into small spaces when applying and wiping off stain. Stain the rest of the piece with desired colors as above. Let dry. (If your piece has any metal parts, paint them with metal paint to coordinate with the stain colors.) Let dry. Apply clear matte sealer to the wood surface.

SCRIPTED *Shelf*

THE CLEVER COMBINATION of water-based colored stain and oil-based artist paint sticks produces stand-out script on an unfinished wood entry shelf. Determine the placement of the lines of text on your shelf by writing out the words to a poem or phrase on a large sheet of paper and arranging the words on the top of the shelf and the drawer fronts. We were able to fit one line of 3-inch-tall text across our drawer fronts. Our shelf was 11 inches deep, so we planned three lines of script for the top. Using a pencil and ruler, mark writing guidelines across the length of the shelf top, spacing them 3½ inches apart. Use transfer paper to transfer your writing from the paper pattern to the shelf, then trace over the writing with a beige oil stick (see photo). (As an alternative to using a pattern, you could freehand the lettering.) Let dry for 24 hours. Next, combine one part teal-colored stain with one part turquoise-colored stain and one part water. (Stains must be water-based. Experiment to create a color that coordinates with your decor.) With a foam brush, apply the stain mixture to the shelf. Wipe away excess stain with a clean rag. The oil-based paint stick will resist the water-based stain, so the words will still be visible. After the shelf has dried for 24 hours, apply a satin-finish sealer that's compatible with the water-based stain. Let dry.

EASY
Additions

54

S

OMETIMES IT JUST TAKES

a little something extra to make your

furniture stand out. Try incorporating

mirrors, wooden appliqués or fresh drawer

pulls or consider entirely unexpected items,

like bottle caps, boards or broken china.

Functional or fanciful, these add-ons pump

up the personality of plain pieces and give

timeworn ones a new lease on life.

56

62

65

VENEER VARIATIONS

VENEERING—The practice of gluing a thin sheet of fine wood to thicker backing for strength.

INLAY—Designs made by cutting a shallow pattern into a wood surfac[e] and filling it with wood of a contrasting color.

MARQUETRY—An ornamental inlay of contrasting woods into a bac[k]ground of veneer.

BOOK MATCHING—Creating a symmetrical pattern by flipping alte[r]nating pieces of veneer so they face each other like pages of a book.

SLIP MATCHING—Joining veneer pieces in sequence without flippi[ng] the pattern so the joints will not be obvious.

HIP TO BE *Square*

1. Measure your tabletop. To ensure a smooth surface, cut a piece of ¾" plywood to fit (or have it cut at a home center). Remove old tabletop. Attach plywood.

2. Plan your design layout on paper. Determine what size squares and number of rows work out evenly for your size tabletop. (For our 20-inch by 36-inch tabletop, we created an 8-inch by 24-inch center rectangle surrounded with three rows of 2-inch squares. For the center rectangle, we used maple veneer; for the squares, we used an alternating pattern of walnut, oak and birch veneers.)

3. Using a carpenters square and pencil, draw the design layout on the new plywood tabletop (see photo A).

4. Draw squares on the back of each variety of 8 ½" x 11" veneer using a pencil and carpenters square. (We used veneer with a high-gloss finish on one side and a low-gloss finish on the other. For the tabletop, we wanted a low-gloss finish, so we placed that side facing up.)

5. Peel back the protective cover paper on one sheet of pressure-sensitive adhesive and lay a veneer sheet, high-gloss side down, directly on top of the adhesive, pressing firmly to transfer the adhesive to the veneer. When you are ready to cut and apply the veneer pieces, peel off the sheet and the adhesive will be on the grid (see photo B). Apply adhesive in the same manner to the gridded sides of the other veneer sheets.

6. On the large sheet of maple veneer, measure and mark the center rectangle. Using a craft knife and carpenters square, cut out the rectangle. If the rectangle is longer than the adhesive sheets, combine full and partial sheets of adhesive to cover it. Apply adhesive as above.

7. Remove the protective backing sheet and position the center rectangle on the tabletop within the guidelines. Press in place.

8. Using scissors, cut apart the small squares a sheet at a time, as needed (see photo C). (Keep adhesive side up and be careful not to overlap the cut squares before placing them on the table; they will stick together.)

9. Beginning at the lower left corner of the table, press the small squares in place, alternating wood tones until the tabletop is covered.

10. Using a craft knife and carpenters square, cut narrow strips from walnut veneer to cover the side edges of the tabletop. (Because we used ¾" plywood, our strips were ¾" wide. Depending on your tabletop measurements and the size of your veneer sheets, you may need to piece together shorter lengths of veneer to cover the space.) Apply adhesive and place in position as above.

11. Seal by spraying with a clear sealer.

SHOPPING LIST

- Old coffee table
- ¾" plywood
- Circular saw
- Carpenters square
- 8 ½" x 11" sheets of high-gloss /low-gloss prefinished veneer in walnut, oak and birch (three sheets of each, plus additional walnut to cover tabletop edges)
- 22" x 24" sheet of high-gloss/ low-gloss prefinished veneer in maple
- Pressure-sensitive veneer adhesive
- Scissors
- Craft knife
- Clear spray sealer
- Tape measure

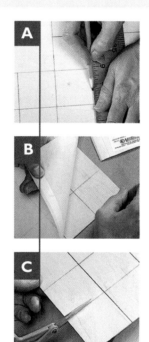

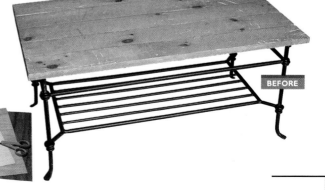

BEFORE

1. Prepare hutch for painting.

2. Paint the hutch, shelves, new decorative trims, new hardware and molding with white latex paint. Let dry.

3. Paint the interior back of the cabinet with robin's-egg blue latex paint. Let dry.

4. Cut pieces of base cap molding to fit around the top, middle and bottom of the hutch, as desired. Use a miter box and backsaw to cut 45-degree angles. Secure moldings with brads or clear construction adhesive. (See box below for tips.)

5. Attach new rosette door handles to doors and carved wood handles to drawers with supplied hardware.

6. Glue trefoil brackets onto the corner edges of each door with construction adhesive. Hold in place with masking tape until dry.

7. Add new wooden feet to bottom of the hutch with supplied hardware.

8. Attach decorative header to top of hutch with construction adhesive and small brads.

9. To subtly decorate the glass doors with a faux-etched design use the trefoil bracket as a pattern. Trace the shape onto a clear self-adhesive plastic laminate sheet and cut it out with an artist knife.

10. Peel off backing and center the stencil pattern on the glass, making sure all the edges are adhered firmly. Apply frosted glass spray paint, following manufacturer's instructions. Let dry and gently peel off the plastic laminate stencil. (To clean the stencil area, use a damp rag. Do not use glass cleaner. The paint can be scraped off with a razor blade if you make a mistake.)

SHOPPING LIST

- Old glass-front cupboard or hutch
- Flat latex paint in white and robin's-egg blue
- Two rosette door handles
- Six carved wood drawer pulls
- Eight wood brackets with trefoil cutouts
- Base cap trim molding
- Four wood feet, bun or finial style
- Gingerbread header
- Miter box
- Backsaw
- Clear construction adhesive
- Small brads
- Frosted glass spray finish
- Craft knife
- Clear self-adhesive plastic laminate
- Masking tape

BEFORE

CUTTING AND ATTACHING MOLDINGS ....

ADDING GINGERBREAD MOLDINGS and decorative trims is the easiest way to give furniture a cottage look without changing its basic shape or structure. Here are some tips for cutting and attaching moldings:

- Attach base cap trim moldings (like those shown around the top, middle and bottom portions of this hutch) to flat surfaces only. Use a miter box with a backsaw to cut 45-degree angles.
- To avoid splitting the wood, predrill holes before attaching moldings; drive brads into the molding with a nail set.
- Use carpenters wood glue or clear construction adhesive to secure moldings where brads cannot be used. Hold the glued pieces together with masking tape or spring clamps until the adhesive dries.

ETCHING WITH STENCILS

WE USED SMALL ROSE CORNER stencils on the tabletop mirror and repeated double rose stencils on each side of the drawer pulls on the drawer-front mirrors. You can also transfer a standard stencil or your own design onto clear, self-adhesive plastic laminate to make a stencil, following the same instructions at right to adhere it and apply etching cream. Do not use regular stencils; they are too thick and will allow etching cream to seep underneath.

REFLECTIVE *Mood*

1. Remove existing knobs from the side table. Measure the tabletop and drawer fronts and have mirror pieces cut to fit each area at a glass/mirror specialty shop. Have holes for the drawer pulls drilled into each piece as well. (We chose two different mirror thicknesses —¼" for the top and ⅛" for the drawers. Use thinner mirror on the drawer fronts so mirror does not stick out too far or come unglued because it's too heavy to stay adhered.)

2. Lightly sand table and wipe with a clean, soft cloth. Using a 2" paintbrush, base-coat table with white primer. Let dry.

3. Using a 2" paintbrush, paint table black. Let dry. Apply a second coat. Let dry.

4. Clean mirror pieces with glass cleaner and dry with paper towels. Determine stencil arrangement on mirror pieces and mark placement using a ruler and small pieces of tape.

5. Begin with one of the small rose corner stencils. Place stencil so waxed backing sheet faces up. (The stencils are made up of a waxed backing sheet, an adhesive layer and a top sheet.) Slowly peel off the entire backing sheet to reveal the adhesive side of the stencil. With the exposed adhesive side facing down, position the stencil over the tape guidelines at the corner of the tabletop mirror. Press in place. Remove the top sheet (see photo A). Repeat to adhere remaining three stencils to the corners of the tabletop mirror.

6. On drawer fronts, for each double rose stencil, peel off backing, position over tape guideline on each side of drawer pull and adhere, removing top sheet after stencil is completely adhered.

7. Once stencils are in place, apply strips of adhesive plastic laminate over the surrounding mirror surface on the tabletop and drawer fronts to protect them from etching cream.

8. Following the diagrams provided with each stencil, remove all indicated stencil sections using tweezers or pins (see photo B). After you have completely removed the stencil pieces from the areas to be etched, place a waxed backing sheet (or a piece of freezer paper if you're using a stencil you made) over the top of each stencil. Rub a burnishing tool across the stencil in both directions to adhere all of the stencil pieces.

9. Using a ½" bristle paintbrush, apply a thick coat of glass-etching cream to stencils (see photo C). Let the cream set for approximately 10 minutes.

10. Wash cream off mirrors. Avoid wetting mirror backs. Remove stencil pieces and adhesive plastic laminate from mirror surfaces. Clean and dry mirrors as before.

11. Apply mirror mastic to tabletop and drawer fronts following manufacturer's instructions. Position the corresponding etched mirrors on tabletop and drawer fronts and press in place. Let dry. Attach new coordinating pulls to drawer fronts through predrilled holes.

SHOPPING LIST

- Side table
- Mirror pieces cut to fit the drawer fronts and the tabletop (available at a glass/mirror specialty shop)
- Sandpaper
- Clean, soft cloth
- White latex primer
- Satin latex paint in black
- 2" paintbrushes
- Glass cleaner
- Paper towels
- Ruler
- Tape
- Glass-etching stencils in small rose corner and double rose patterns
- Clear self-adhesive plastic laminate
- Tweezers and straight pins
- Freezer paper
- Burnishing tool
- ½" bristle paintbrush
- Glass-etching cream
- Mirror mastic
- Glass drawer pulls

A

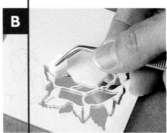

B

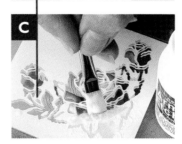

C

BEFORE

1. Remove the hardware, including the door hinges and knobs for the drawer fronts and doors, from your furniture piece. Remove door panels. (Our cupboard had removeable punched-copper panels. If your piece has wood panels that cannot easily be removed, you may need to cut out the panels with a jigsaw. Use a drill to make a pilot hole in one corner of the panel before cutting.)

2. Prepare surface for painting.

3. Spray-paint the cupboard outside or in a well-ventilated area. Protect surfaces from overspray with newspapers or drop cloths. It is a good idea to wear a dust mask. (Test the spray paint first in a hidden spot. The lacquer in spray paints can cause certain finishes to wrinkle. If this is the case, switch to a compatible brush-on paint or seal the surface with an all-purpose primer before applying the base coat.)

4. Holding the can upright 12 to 16 inches from the surface, spray in a back-and-forth motion to cover the cupboard with paint (see photo A). Use light, even strokes, slightly overlapping each stroke. Apply two or more light coats, letting dry for a few minutes between coats. Avoid spraying too heavily in one spot, which may cause the paint to drip and run. Let dry overnight. (This treatment involves distressing this white top coat to reveal portions of the base coat. If you are not happy with the existing color of your piece, base-coat it the desired color with flat latex paint and let dry before applying the white paint.)

5. In random areas, use 100- or 120-grit sandpaper to distress the surface of the cabinet by lightly sanding through the newly painted surface to reveal the base coat below (see photo B). Pay extra attention to areas that might naturally receive wear and tear, including the edges of doors or drawers, corners and trim details. In some areas, such as around the doors and on the top and sides of the cupboard, drag the sandpaper across the surface to scuff it. Wipe with a tack cloth.

6. Use the old panels as a guide to determine size of replacement panels. Allow excess wire cloth to fully fit the framework of door, with room to staple. Use tin snips to cut wire cloth to size (see photo C).

7. Spray the wire cloth with white paint to match the cupboard or leave unpainted. When dry, staple in place to the back inside of the door frames using ¼" staples.

8. Replace the hardware and hinges to coordinate with the style of the room. (We used decorator pulls with a kitchen theme to fit in with other cabinetry in our room.)

TIP: *Chicken wire, embossed-tin ceiling panels and frosted glass also will give a piece like this an updated look.*

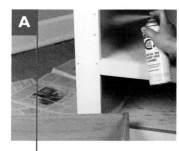

A

B

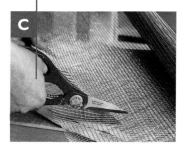

C

BEFORE

BISCUITS

WEATHERED *Wood*

SHOPPING LIST

- Nightstand or other furniture piece
- Found pieces of distressed, painted beadboard (available at salvage yards, flea markets or at the curb on garbage day)
- Backsaw or saber saw
- 150-grit sandpaper
- Clear construction adhesive
- Clamps
- Clear matte sealer

1. Remove drawers from your piece and take off drawer pulls. Prepare surface for painting. (Our piece was prefinished. If your piece is unfinished, prime and paint it as desired.)

2. Gather old pieces of painted, weathered and distressed beadboard to cover desired area on your piece. Look for pieces that are all the same thickness. (The thinner the wood, the more natural the finished drawer will look.)

BEFORE

3. Cut the pieces with a backsaw or saber saw to fit the front of each drawer. It is more interesting if the boards are pieced together, so cut some short and fill in. The edges of the beadboard pieces should be flush with the edges of the drawer front—any overhang may cause problems with the drawer operation. (You can also use this treatment on door panels or the open back of a hutch.)

4. Lightly sand edges of boards to remove peeling or flaking paint (see photo A). To prevent more paint from flaking off, apply a matte-finish sealer to the boards.

5. Place drawers on end, with fronts facing up. Apply construction adhesive to the backs of the boards and adhere them to the drawer fronts (see photo B). Clamp in place until set.

6. Replace drawer pulls. (You may need to use longer screws due to the added depth of the wood.)

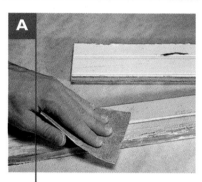
A

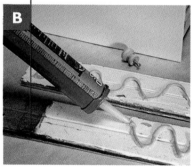
B

SELECTING WOOD

CHOOSE DISCARDED WOOD for its colors and distressed qualities. If you can't find distressed wood, just stain, sand, paint and distress new pieces. You can even mix the new with the old to stretch a small supply. As an alternative to beadboard, you can select an assortment of old wood trim pieces. For a finished look, consider framing the wood with mitered pieces of stained pine drip cap molding.

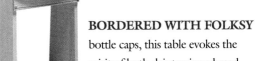

POP *Art*

BORDERED WITH FOLKSY bottle caps, this table evokes the spirit of both dainty gingerbread trim and whimsical tramp art. Originally made between 1875 and 1930, tramp art pieces—often created with scavenged materials—feature fancy, layered detailing. Use this idea on various furniture pieces or even small accessories. (For nonwood items, use hot glue to attach caps.) Prime piece with white spray primer. Collect bottle caps or purchase them from a home-brew supplier. Determine the placement of the nails on the bottle caps. For our design, we placed nails near the top edges of some caps, including those around the tabletop. This allows them to hang over the edge of the table, creating a decorative scallop. On flat surfaces, such as the face of the table legs and the sides of the table, we placed nails through the cap centers. With an awl or nail punch, make small dents in the flat surface of the caps. This dent will hold the sharp tip of the nail in place and keep it from slipping as you tap the nail through the top of the bottle cap. Working on a scrap board, tap nails through dents in caps using a hammer (see photo). Attach the pre-nailed bottle caps along the vertical and horizontal edges and other areas on the table. Spray entire piece with two coats of white enamel spray paint following manufacturer's instructions. Spray with sealer.

GARDEN GRIPS

MOUNT GARDEN TOOLS on the fronts of cabinet doors to add to the theme of a garden room and act as handles. Purchase a pair of secondhand long-handled garden tools and paint the wood handles with bright green latex or acrylic paint. Plan placement of the tools on the door fronts. We centered our tools on the panels, placing the bottom edges of the tools 3 inches from the bottom edges of the doors. We mounted the tools with 3" screws, each equipped with a spacer to create room between the handle and the door. To create spacers, cut pieces of 5/16" round brass tubing with a hacksaw and paint them to match the tool handles using green spray paint for metal surfaces. To attach the tools, place a screw-and-spacer set near the top of each tool and a second one near the bottom. Mark desired points on handles and use a small bit to prestart holes and prevent handles from splitting when mounting. To mount the handles, mark corresponding points on door fronts and drill pilot holes for the screws. Next, carefully drive 3" screws though the door from the inside, placing the appropriate spacers on the screws as they emerge. Align screw tips with prestarted holes on handles. Continue driving the screws into the tool until both screws are secure.

BITS
& Pieces

PIECES OF BROKEN CHINA create a mosaic design on a nightstand. The technique works best on a furniture piece with an inset area, like this cabinet. Prepare the surface for painting, then base-coat the cabinet top and door frame with peach paint. Paint the rest of the piece with vanilla paint. To soften the peach areas, dry brush over them with vanilla. Wrap pieces of old china (we used about three dinner plates to have enough patterned pieces to choose from) within a protective fabric, like an old towel or pillowcase. Use a hammer to break the dishes into small pieces until you have shapes you like. (Wear goggles to protect your eyes.) Choose broken pieces with patterns and shapes that will fill the cabinet door inset panel, creating a balanced design. We allowed approximately $1/16$ inch to $1/8$ inch between the pieces. Continue breaking china as needed until you have enough shapes and sizes to create the desired design. For more control, use tile nippers to create desired shapes. Glue pieces in place using construction adhesive (see photo). With a plastic trowel, thoroughly work white premixed mosaic grout in the spaces between the china pieces until the entire mosaic area is covered. If necessary, smooth uneven joints with your fingers. Wipe excess grout from the surface of the china with a sponge. Allow the grout to set according to manufacturer's instructions (about 15 minutes), then wipe surface and smooth joints again with a slightly damp rag or sponge. Finish cleaning the surface with a dry rag. Let grout dry thoroughly. Add a coordinating knob to the piece for a finishing touch.

PEEKABOO PLATTER

ADORN A SIDE TABLE with a glimmering crystal panel. We used a salvaged sewing machine table and an old-fashioned platter. Make a pattern of the back of the platter's center portion, not including the rim. Transfer the pattern to the table. Cut out the shape with a jigsaw, cutting to the inside of the outline to ensure the hole will not be too large. You can always enlarge the hole, if needed. Paint the table white. Secure the rim of the platter to the inside of the table with construction adhesive or screwed-in mirror clips.

WOVEN *Veneer*

ADD A LITTLE PRIMITIVE COUNTRY STYLE to a plain armoire with woven strips of veneer edging. Remove doors from the armoire and lay flat. Measure the length and width of the door panels that will be covered with veneer strips. Cut strips of 7/8" pre-glued, iron-on veneer edging to the appropriate length and lay them side by side until they cover the width of the panels. With thumbtacks, tack each veneer strip at the top to the door panel. Cut more veneer strips to the width of the panels (enough so when woven into the longer strips they will cover the entire surface). Stain these strips with black (or other desired color) wood stain. Slide the shorter strips into the longer strips attached to the door panel. On the first row, start by weaving under the first strip and over the next. Alternate each row to achieve a checkerboard effect (see photo). When the entire door panel is woven, tack down the other end of the veneer strips with thumbtacks to hold the entire weave to the surface. To bond the weave to the door panel, start by preheating an iron to the "cotton" setting. Cover woven surface with kraft paper or aluminum foil and slowly press the iron over the veneer until glue melts and creates a bond to the door. While veneer is still hot, press it firmly with a wood block or roller. Finish off the edges of the veneer by framing it with a thin piece of decorative molding and small brads. Top-coat the entire surface with clear matte sealer.

LEAFY *Appliqués*

FRENCH COUNTRY FURNITURE is often adorned with simple carving or handpainted details. Decorative wood appliqués make it easy to create a similar look on a plain furniture piece, like this basic buffet. First, we aged the buffet by using a candle wax resist technique, sanding away the white top coat in selected areas to reveal a spring green base coat (see page 122 for more on resist techniques). Plan and mark the layout of the wood appliqués on the buffet front. We used leaf- and flower-shaped appliqués. You can combine them to create different shapes. We centered one leaf appliqué horizontally on each drawer front, with the center leaves facing down. On the center of each door, we paired two leaf appliqués, placing them vertically, with the center leaves facing out and the edges touching. We placed a small flower appliqué in the center to cover the gap between the appliqués. We also added four small flower appliqués to the four outside corners of the buffet. Base-coat all appliqués with the same base color (spring green) as the buffet. Let dry. Using a stencil brush, dab dark leaf green stencil cream on the center of an appliqué, working it into the grooves and ridges. Rub with a paper towel to remove excess cream and allow the base coat to show through in some areas. On the ends of the appliqué, apply medium leaf green stencil cream as above. Let dry. Use white stencil cream to highlight random areas on the appliqué, such as the edges of the center section and the leaf tips. With paper towel, gently dab off some white cream so you can still see it as a highlight over the green. Complete all appliqués in this manner. When they are dry, top-coat with clear matte sealer. Use clear construction adhesive to adhere the appliqués to the buffet at the marked points.

MAGIC MIRROR

Create an elegant accent piece by topping a small table with a gilded-frame mirror. Start with a round accent table and find a mirror with a gilded frame that is just slightly bigger than the tabletop. (If you have difficulty finding a round mirror to fit, buy a round frame in the proper dimensions and order a mirror to fit from a glass shop. Look for a wide wood frame; it may be difficult to insert screws into plastic or plaster frames.) Mask off the mirror with tape, then base-coat the table and frame with cream-colored paint. Let the base coat dry, then dry brush gold metallic paint over the surface of the table and mirror until desired effect is achieved. Let dry. Set framed mirror on tabletop and determine best location for screws, which will hold the two pieces together. Place screws so they are centered between the legs along the edge of the table and a thick part of the frame. It is best to predrill pilot holes through the tabletop. Hold the frame in place on the tabletop and use the holes in the tabletop to mark the back of the frame for predrilling. Do not drill all the way through the frame. Align pilot holes on the two pieces. Carefully drive screws into the predrilled holes from the underside of the table up into the frame, making sure the frame does not shift by clamping it in place. Continue until all screws are secured and the mirror back is flush against the tabletop. Touch up with paint.

SPECIAL *Effects*

70

72

74

78

THERE ARE MANY TECHNIQUES

that replicate the look of a certain surface

or material, from polished malachite to

burled wood. Paint and a few simple tools

are all you need to create faux finishes that

give plain pieces luxe looks. Though it may

take some practice, the techniques are easy

enough for a beginner to master, and the

results are simply stunning.

WATER *Droplets*

1. Remove hardware from chest. Base-coat the entire piece with antique white paint. Let dry. (If you are using this technique on a piece with an existing finish, prepare it properly before base-coating.)

2. Place the drawer on a flat surface with the front facing up to avoid drips. (Work on one drawer at a time, proceeding immediately to the next step, because the alcohol will not react with the paint in the proper manner if it is dry.)

3. Lightly spray the center area on the face of the drawer with water and quickly paint the surface with a light coat of fern green using a foam brush (see photo A). The water thins the paint slightly. (Instead of spraying the surface with water and then painting over it, you can use a colorwash. Just mix equal parts of fern paint and water.)

4. Using a dry chip brush, lightly sweep the bristle tips across the surface to smooth paint and create a more uniform finish.

5. Wearing rubber gloves to protect your hands, immediately drip denatured alcohol onto the surface while the paint is still wet (see photo B), using a cotton swab or dripping directly from the can. For a "drop-within-a-drop" look, drip alcohol in the same spot several times. Work in a well-ventilated area. Let dry for 30 minutes to an hour.

6. If desired, use a narrow foam brush and antique white paint to touch up edges around technique area. Seal the entire piece to protect the finish. Reattach the hardware.

SHOPPING LIST

- Unfinished lingerie chest
- Semigloss latex paint in antique white
- Flat latex paint in fern green
- Satin-finish sealer
- 1 pint of denatured alcohol solvent
- Rubber gloves
- Cotton swabs
- Foam brushes
- Chip brush

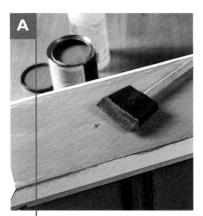

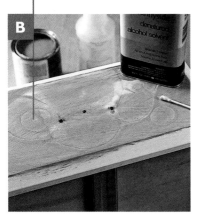

INSTANT REACTION

WHEN ALCOHOL TOUCHES a freshly painted surface, the paint pigment migrates to the edges of the droplet to produce a ringed look. Combining a flat top coat and a semigloss base coat supplies the perfect surface for this surprising reaction. Use two paint colors in the same family for a subtle look, or layer contrasting colors to kick the drama up a notch.

TIP: *Instead of dripping the alcohol, you can use a long-bristled brush to spatter the surface. Wearing rubber gloves, dip the brush into the alcohol and bend back the bristles of the brush with your fingers.*

TORTOISESHELL *Table*

- Wooden end table
- 150-grit sandpaper
- Tack cloth
- White latex primer
- 4" foam roller
- Acrylic craft paint in metallic gold
- Two 3" foam paintbrushes
- Clear matte sealer
- Foam plates
- Acrylic craft paint in raw sienna, burnt sienna and burnt umber
- Gallon-size reclosable plastic storage bags
- Three 1" paintbrushes
- Softening brush
- Paper towel
- Glaze base
- Paint-spattering brush or two artist paintbrushes

1. Sand your wood surface lightly, going in the direction of the grain, and wipe with a tack cloth. Apply a coat of latex primer. Let dry, then sand lightly, again wiping away dust with a tack cloth.

2. With a 4" foam roller, base-coat piece metallic gold. Let dry.

3. With a 3" foam brush, apply two coats of sealer. Let dry.

4. On separate foam plates, mix each acrylic paint color with an equal amount of glaze and seal each plate in a reclosable plastic bag.

5. Beginning with the raw sienna glaze mixture, use a 1" paintbrush to apply a series of diagonal oblong shapes with space between them (see photo A).

6. Let glaze set up slightly for approximately 2 to 5 minutes, checking a small area of paint in a corner for readiness. Move the brush back and forth in the same diagonal direction as before, with just the tips of the brush touching the surface, to gently mute color and soften brush strokes (see photo B). If you're dragging the color beyond the brush stroke, the glaze needs more drying time. When glaze is ready, go over the previous brush strokes. Use cross strokes to further soften the original strokes. (If the glaze mixture dries too quickly, add more straight glaze during application.) Let dry.

7. Apply a coat of sealer. Let dry. (Sealing after each color application allows you to wipe away mistakes in the next layer without affecting previously applied colors.)

8. Add small patches of burnt sienna glaze mixture, following the direction of the first shapes so they slightly overlap. Soften, blend and seal as in Step 6 and Step 7. Let dry.

9. Add larger quantities of burnt umber glaze mixture following the diagonal direction of the paint, again touching and running alongside previously applied glazes. Soften, blend and seal as in Step 6 and Step 7. Let dry.

10. Load a spattering brush with burnt umber glaze mixture. Working close to the surface, place a fine spattering over open areas by pulling the bristles back with your finger (see photo C). Let set, then soften as in Step 6. Let dry. Apply a coat of sealer.

11. Step back and look at the tortoiseshell surface to view the overall effect. Add glaze colors where needed, using the techniques above. Let dry. Apply two coats of sealer, letting dry in between.

SHELL GAME

THOUGH USING REAL TORTOISESHELL as a veneer is now illegal, you can create the pattern by painting strokes and spots of varying widths and lengths in a diagonal direction. Colors vary but often include shades of gold, brown and black. We applied acrylic paints and glazes over a gold metallic base to add a tortoiseshell pattern to a custom-cut piece of 1/4" plywood, which we used to replace a glass tabletop.

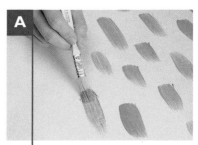

TIP: *Instead of using a spattering brush, you can load an artist brush with paint and gently tap the brush handle with another brush to spatter the paint.*

A REAL *Gem*

1. Fill holes on wood piece. Sand until smooth and wipe with tack cloth. (The surface should be very even as this technique highlights imperfections as well as wood grain. Because of our cabinet's construction, we faux-finished smooth ⅜"-thick boards and cut them to fit within the cabinet's framework.)

2. Apply primer and let dry. If you plan to use the malachite finish on selected areas, mask them off and plan to paint the remaining areas later.

3. Base-coat the areas of the piece where you wish to create the finish with blue-green. Let dry.

4. Tear an irregularly shaped 3-inch piece of corrugated cardboard, leaving the torn edge of the top paper layer attached.

5. Mix equal parts of viridian green and glaze base. Apply glaze mixture over the base coat with a foam brush (see photo A). To ensure a consistent finish, coat the entire surface of each area, such as the cabinet top, at one time.

6. Let glaze set up. Starting at the center of the area, work in irregular semicircles, holding cardboard at a 45-degree angle with the torn edge down (see photo B). Pull cardboard through glaze with a slight wiggle, pivoting from one corner in the center. (If background color is strong, brush out glaze, let sit for a few minutes and start again.) Allow each semicircle to overlap slightly. Tear and use new pieces of cardboard as old ones become clogged with paint. Use different sizes for variation.

7. Go over the pattern with a softening brush, using cross strokes to further soften. (If the glaze mixture dries too quickly, add more straight glaze during softening.) Let dry.

8. Use a ¼" flat artist brush or your fingertip to add whorls in select gaps between the swirls (see photo C). Let dry. Apply sealer to protect finish.

SHOPPING LIST

- Furniture piece
- Wood filler
- Sandpaper
- Tack cloth
- White latex primer
- Foam brush
- Flat latex paint in blue-green
- Paintbrush
- Glaze base
- Artist acrylic in viridian green
- Corrugated cardboard
- Softening brush
- ¼" flat artist brush
- Clear matte sealer

A

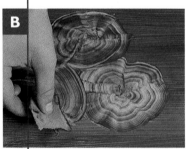

B

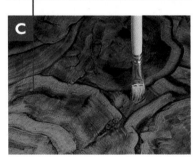

C

MALACHITE MAGIC .....

A SEMIPRECIOUS STONE

distinctive for its color and circular and ribbonlike patterns, malachite gets its name from the Greek word "mallow," in reference to its green leaf color. Though it can be pale green, it is generally a deep jade with blue overtones. It's stunning on small pieces, like frames and boxes, as well as larger items, like this cabinet. Since the finish is sheer, it's best to use it on very smooth or finely grained surfaces.

FAUX-ETCHED *Glass*

SHOPPING LIST

- Table base with a removable round glass tabletop
- Clear self-adhesive plastic laminate
- Scissors
- Burnishing tool
- Kraft paper
- Masking tape
- Heat stencil-cutting tool
- Frosted glass spray finish
- Craft knife
- Four vinyl surface protectors

1. Clean the tabletop. Cut a piece of self-adhesive plastic laminate to fit the tabletop and smooth it in place, using a burnishing tool to press out any air bubbles. If the plastic laminate is not wide enough to cover your tabletop, use two pieces, placing them edge to edge to cover the surface. Set the tabletop aside.

2. From kraft paper, cut a round template the size of your tabletop. Fold the template into quarters. Unfold. The creases will divide the template into quadrants, which will help you determine stencil placement.

3. Create your own stencil design or use or adapt a design from ready-made stencils. Choose or design a pattern that works well with the shape of your tabletop.

4. Make four photocopies of your stencil design. Enlarge each of them to fit inside a quadrant of the paper template. Tape a photocopy in each quadrant. Trim edge to fit rounded shape of the paper template.

5. Place the template, design side up, on a flat work surface. Place the glass round, plastic laminate side up, on the template. Use the heat stencil-cutting tool tip to cut the stencil design from the plastic laminate. Peel away the cutout shapes as you work (see photo A). After completing the entire design, make sure all cut edges are adhered firmly to the glass to prevent spray paint from leaking under the stencil. Also, add a strip of masking tape to cover the seam between the pieces of plastic laminate.

6. Following manufacturer's instructions, hold the spray paint can 10 to 12 inches above the surface and apply over the design area using a steady back and forth motion (see photo B). Don't apply spray too heavily, as build-up can yellow. Instead, apply several thin coats of spray, letting dry between coats. Let dry overnight after the final coat.

7. Lift and peel the plastic laminate away from the glass (see photo C), using an artist knife if needed.

8. Place vinyl surface protectors on top of the metal table base to prevent scratching the frosted design.

9. With the tabletop turned so the design is on the underside, set it in place atop the base. After letting the paint cure for about a week, clean the design area with glass cleaner, if needed.

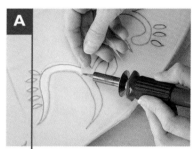

A

B

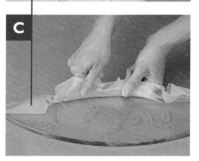

C

SIMPLY PRETTY . . . .

THERE ARE MANY PRODUCTS that can produce a chemically etched surface, but the advantage of this spray paint method is that it's much simpler. You can use it on any glass or mirror surface, from cabinet doors to decorative accessories, to add elegantly etched detailing.

PAPER *Mosaic*

MIMIC THE LOOK OF GLASS MOSAIC using torn bits of paper to make a patterned tabletop. Prepare the surface for painting, and apply white primer. Let dry. Dry brush the surface with gray acrylic paint, varying the application. This creates the appearance of grout between the paper "tiles." Transfer or trace a pattern outline onto the tabletop. Choose a simple design, like our fish with a wave border. Hand-dye rice paper with thinned acrylic paints. (You can also use colored tissue paper, but it will not have the mottled effect and color variation of the dyed paper.) To create dye solutions, mix one part paint to three parts water in small containers. (Vary the ratio depending on the color saturation desired.) Mix one solution for each color. Test dye a few pieces of paper to ensure you like the colors. (When the paper is dry, it should appear mottled, with lighter and darker sections.) Tear the paper into strips that fit into the dye containers and dip the strips, allowing excess dye to drip back into the container. Dry flat on a wire rack. Dye paper strips until you have enough of each color. When the paper is dry, tear it into small pieces. Sizes and shapes should vary. Do not tear up all dyed paper; set some aside for tearing pieces to fit larger areas or unusual spaces. Divide by color. Working on one section of tabletop at a time, apply a bit of decoupage medium with your finger or a small brush to one side of a paper piece (see photo). Place onto table in desired area. Fill in around it, evenly distributing values of the same color. Leave 1/16 inch to 1/8 inch between pieces. Fill in each area with appropriate colors. Let dry. Seal tabletop with a coat of decoupage medium. Have glass cut to fit the tabletop to further protect the finish.

BURLED WOOD

A FROTTAGE TECHNIQUE recreates the look of burled wood on a small side table. Frottage, which means rubbing, is an age-old art technique that has been adapted by decorative painters. It involves applying a glaze to a base-coated surface, then blotting or dabbing with a sheet material, such as plastic, paper or cloth, to create a texture or pattern. Prepare the furniture surface for painting, then base-coat with flat medium-gold paint. Let dry. Brush brown-tinted glaze over a section of the table with a 2" chip brush. (Because our tabletop was small, we were able to do the entire surface at one time. For larger pieces, work on small sections, about 24 inches square, so you can complete the technique before the glaze dries.) Crumple a piece of plastic wrap and use it to lift off some of the wet glaze. Replace wrap as it gets overloaded. Tap the wet glaze with your fingertip several times within a small area to replicate the bull's-eye effect seen in real wood (see photo). Let dry. To create a border pattern around the piece,

measure in 1 inch and mask off the area with painters tape. Adjust or fold tape to fit curved edges. Working in 6-inch sections, apply another coat of glaze to the border. Fold a small piece of paper and use the edge to dab the wet glaze, creating a darker striped design. Carefully remove tape. Let dry. Apply glaze to legs and other sections of the table and lift off with plastic wrap as above. Let dry. Coat with clear sealer.

GIVE A SMOOTH, unfinished cabinet a more rugged look with corrugated cardboard and glaze. We used the treatment on a bathroom vanity cabinet. Base-coat the cabinet with cream paint using a 4" foam roller. Let dry. Mix one part terra-cotta paint with two parts glaze and pour into a paint tray. Using a 1" foam brush, smoothly apply an even coat of glaze to the portions of the cabinet that will not have the grain effect. (On our cabinet, we did this on the legs and the raised areas framing the panels.) Let dry. Measure the areas where you wish to apply the grain effect and use a craft knife and metal ruler to cut rectangles of corrugated cardboard to fit. Mark the back of each cardboard piece with the corresponding area on the cabinet for reference. Lightly spray the ribbed surface of the cardboard with water to increase absorbency. Press and flatten different sections of the ribbed surface so it will leave a more uneven pattern on the glazed surface. Beginning with one section, apply a coat of terra-cotta glaze using a 4" foam roller. While glaze is still wet, lay the appropriate prepared cardboard piece over the glazed section, ribbed side down. Press firmly, starting at the top and working to the bottom in vertical sections. The harder you press, the more glaze will be lifted. Peel back a corner of the cardboard to check imprint (see photo). If not satisfied with a section, reapply glaze and repeat. Complete the remainder of the cabinet. Once paint is dry, apply a coat of clear sealer.

ROUGH *Hewn*

INSTANT *Artistry*

82

84

86

HOME FURNISHINGS SHOPS and boutiques are filled with beautiful (and pricey) handpainted furniture. To recreate this look for a whole lot less—no painting skill required—try your hand at decoupage and image-transfer techniques. Whether you apply a premade art imprint or a pretty bloom snipped from gift wrap, you can quickly and easily add an artistic touch to a plain piece.

92

RTA RESCUE

THE POPULARITY OF ready-to-assemble furniture allows home-owners to purchase substantial pieces, like this pine buffet, at affordable prices. Though these pieces are often bereft of decoration, the low price tag allows you to feel more comfortable experimenting with various finish techniques to suit your style. Here, we painted the piece white and added floral stencils topped with glazed tissue paper for an antique look. Most treatments will work, except staining and heat transfer, which call for a raw wood surface.

TISSUE-PAPER *Texture*

1. Prepare surface and base-coat piece with white paint. Let dry.

2. On the two outer cabinet doors, we oriented the stencil the same way; on the middle door, we flipped it. With pencil, mark order of placement (left, middle, right) on top back of doors to help you orient them properly when stenciling. Remove doors from buffet.

3. For the left and right doors, place the first stencil overlay on the bottom left-hand corner of the cabinet inset panel. Make sure the stencil overlay lines up with each side of the inset panel and registration marks. Secure the overlay using painters tape, making sure it lines up evenly with the left bottom corner.

4. Stencil the right and left doors using separate stencil brushes for each color (see photo A). Use blue for the flowers and green for the stems and leaves or a combination of colors that suits your room. Let dry. Continue to stencil the right and left doors using the second and third overlays, securing them as above, letting the paint dry between each overlay.

5. To stencil the middle door, clean the stencil and flip it over so it is a mirror image of the right and left doors. Place the first stencil overlay on the bottom right-hand corner of the inset panel above. (We left the beveled area on the door white and covered the rest of the door with the tissue technique.) Tear tissue into pieces of varying sizes and crumple, then pat down and smooth out with a burnishing tool. The paper should have a wrinkled texture. Starting from the left corner of a panel, place a small amount of decoupage medium on the inset panel with a sponge brush. Place pieces of tissue on the decoupage medium

and pat down, making sure they are wrinkled with crevices but are not bubbly (see photo B). (Be careful not to get any decoupage medium in beveled areas; it will be hard to remove later.) Continue with this process until the entire inset panel is covered. Repeat for the remaining portion of the door and the other doors.

6. When decoupage medium is dry to the touch, use a craft knife to score or tear the paper around the edges of the inset panel and door border to remove portions of the tissue paper that extend beyond the edges.

7. Coat the tissue paper with decoupage medium and let dry.

8. Apply two coats of sealer to the tissue paper, allowing it to dry between coats. The sealer prevents paint from darkly staining the tissue paper. Let dry overnight.

9. Mix equal parts yellow ochre artist acrylic and glaze. Apply yellow glaze to the top of the tissue using a dry brush. As with the tissue paper, work on one small area at a time. Let glaze sit for about 1 minute, then wipe off, using a paper towel, leaving paint in the crevices of the crinkled tissue paper (see photo C). Some areas may have more crevices and some may be smooth. For an uneven aged look, apply more glaze in the crevices than in the smooth areas. Use a baby wipe to clean off excess glaze.

10. Tape off the border around the top of the buffet and the border at the bottom of the buffet. Apply glaze mixture to these areas as above. In some areas, wipe away enough that the white paint shows through. Apply glaze to drawer pulls as well. Seal the entire piece.

SHOPPING LIST

- Pine buffet
- White latex paint
- Paintbrush
- Trumpet vine stencil
- Painters tape
- Acrylic craft paint in periwinkle blue and sage green
- Two stencil brushes
- White tissue paper
- Burnishing tool
- Decoupage medium
- Sponge brush
- Craft knife
- Matte brush-on sealer
- Glaze base
- Artist acrylic in yellow ochre
- Paper towels
- Baby wipes

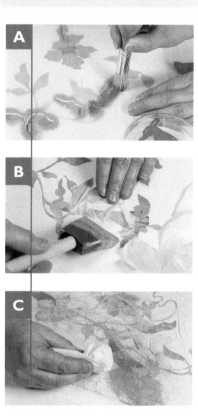

BEFORE

1. Remove seat cushion from chair (or cover with plastic). Prepare surface for painting and prime.

2. Base-coat chair with three coats of off-white paint. Let dry.

3. Use a stencil and medium yellow craft paint to stencil a checkerboard design on the back splat and around the seat apron of the chair. Let dry for 24 hours.

4. Plan your imprint design. We applied a single iris to the back splat and an iris to each chair leg and the base of the arms. We also added butterfly imprints to the legs, arms and chair back.

5. Coat the entire chair with sealer for uniformity. (Imprints work best on a smooth, well-sealed surface, so you may need to apply several coats.) Let dry.

6. With a foam brush, apply imprint adhesive coat in the areas where you plan to place the imprints. Brush in all directions to thoroughly cover the surface. Let set for 15 to 30 minutes or until it is tacky. (The imprint adhesive is effective for as long as it remains tacky, approximately 2 hours.)

7. Using scissors, trim the imprint to within ½ inch of the image. (Keep the protective cover sheet in place to prevent damage to the imprint.) Lay the image facedown on the surface at the preplanned location and tape in place. (To apply imprints to curved surfaces, you may have to snip the imprint paper in several places along the edges or even cut it in half to keep the edges from curling. You can always paint over an imprint if you make a mistake.)

8. Rub the craft stick onto the surface using a small circular motion to transfer the imprint. Gently lift the edge of the imprint to check progress (see photo A). Replace imprint and rub until image is complete. Remove tape and lift off backing.

9. Apply a coat of sealer to the entire piece to seal the imprint and neutralize the imprint coat.

10. Cover the seat cushion with coordinating yellow-and-white checked fabric, if desired.

SHOPPING LIST

- Old or unfinished chair (ours was a Queen Anne style)
- Plastic drop cloth (optional)
- Sandpaper
- Off-white latex paint and primer
- Paintbrush
- Gingham/checkerboard stencil
- Acrylic craft paint in medium yellow
- Stencil brush
- Butterflies and iris imprints
- Imprint adhesive coat
- Clear matte sealer
- Foam brush
- Scissors
- Wood craft stick
- Yellow-and-white checked fabric (optional)

A

BEFORE

TIP: *If you'd like to give the chair an aged look with a glaze or antiquing medium or distress the wood surface, do so either before the initial coat of sealer or after the imprint has been applied and sealed.*

WHAT IS AN IMPRINT?

IMPRINTING IS A PROCESS whereby an artistic image (painted by a professional artist) is reproduced and processed onto special paper, which releases the imprint onto an adhesive coat that has been applied to a piece of furniture. The imprint is rubbed off onto the treated furniture and sealed in place with a finish coat. The result is a clean image that actually looks like handpainting, not a decal.

SIGNS OF *Spring*

1. Prepare dresser for painting.

2. Base-coat dresser with light tan paint using a foam brush. Let dry.

3. Mix one part lavender paint with two parts glaze base. Apply glaze mixture to the dresser top and edges of the dresser frame using a foam brush (see photo A). Let glaze dry.

4. Before cutting, plan layout of wallpaper patterns and the size and placement of cutouts to showcase designs. For interest, use background paper on every other drawer and border paper on drawers in between. For design continuity, center the patterns vertically and horizontally in the same manner on each drawer front. This will help you place the cutouts later. (We cut individual floral diamond shapes from the border paper and centered them over the background paper's vertical stripes. We also aligned these with flowers on the border-covered drawers.)

5. Calculate the number of cutouts needed for the dresser sides and the drawer fronts.

6. Cut pieces of wallpaper to fit drawer fronts and dresser sides. Protect your work surface with a self-healing cutting board, and cut wallpaper with a carpenters square and craft knife, making sure to match the pattern repeat.

7. Cut out wallpaper motifs that will be showcased with a carpenters square and craft knife as above. The size of the diamonds or motifs on the drawer fronts may need to be slightly different from those on the dresser sides. (For example, we used 8½-inch by 5-inch diamonds on the drawer fronts and 8⅛-inch by 5⅜-inch diamonds on the dresser sides.)

8. Apply the prepasted plaid and border wallpapers to the drawer fronts and sides of dresser using water, a sponge and a wallpaper brush, following manufacturer's instructions (see photo B). (For nonpasted paper, use wallpaper adhesive or decoupage medium for application.) Let dry.

9. To attach the floral diamond cutouts or other cutout motifs, use a vinyl-on-vinyl adhesive, following manufacturer's instructions. Be sure to carefully center and align each cutout (see photo C). Let dry. (If you are not using vinyl wallcoverings, follow your wallcovering manufacturer's instructions for adhesive usage.)

10. Use a foam brush to apply a coat of clear matte sealer to the entire piece.

11. Attach coordinating drawer pulls.

VERY CHERRY ....

FOR A VARIATION, pair plaid wallpaper with cherry stencils. Follow the instructions above to mix and apply sage green glaze and green-and-white plaid wallpaper pieces. Determine number and placement of cherry stencils on each drawer front and mark with pencil. Spray the back of the stencil with repositionable adhesive and place on one end of drawer front. Use stencil brushes to apply medium leaf green to the leaves and cherry red to the fruit. Vary the heaviness of paint application for interest. On the cherries, use a lighter application of paint and circular brush strokes to create rounded highlights. Let dry. Reposition the stencil and continue adding designs to complete all drawer fronts. Protect the finish with clear matte sealer and add decorative pulls.

SHOPPING LIST
- Dresser
- Sandpaper and tack cloth
- Glaze base
- Flat latex paint in light tan and lavender
- Foam brushes
- Prepasted plaid wallpaper
- Prepasted floral wallpaper border
- Craft knife
- Carpenters square
- Self-healing cutting board
- Wallpaper tray
- Wallpaper brush
- Vinyl-on-vinyl adhesive
- Sponge
- Clear matte sealer
- Decorative drawer pulls

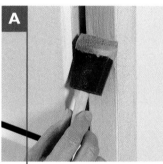

A

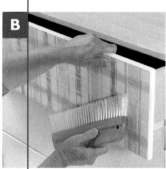

B

C

RECIPE *Table*

1. Paint the table with two coats of seafoam green paint. Let dry between coats.

2. Cut a large rectangular piece of butcher paper and determine the size of recipe card that works best with your table shape and size. For our 36-inch by 44 ½-inch table, we made a 20-inch by 31-inch paper template.

3. Determine the placement of the recipe on the table. We placed it diagonally over the center of the table. Using a ruler and pencil, mark placement on the table (see photo A).

4. Using a computer, determine the desired font style and layout of the recipe and select clip-art images of baking-related items.

5. Print out recipe and use a standard copy machine to enlarge the design. You may have to enlarge the design in sections several times to achieve the desired size of the text and clip art. Assemble sections onto the paper template, adjusting spacing and placement. Use spray-mount adhesive to attach the recipe sections to the paper.

6. To create a one-piece version of the enlarged recipe, take the assembled template to a copy store with a blueprint machine. (This machine prints on large rolls of paper; trim the final copy to desired size using a straightedge and craft knife.)

7. Using colored pencils, color the graphics on the recipe with red and green.

8. Using Glossy Wood Tone spray paint, lightly and evenly spray the recipe to give it an aged feel (see photo B).

9. To create the painted border on the table, first apply ½" painters tape along the pencil outline, then add a row of ¼" tape and a final row of ½" tape. Remove the ¼" tape, leaving a space for the red border.

10. Using red craft paint and a ½" foam brush, fill in the border (see photo C). Remove tape.

11. Using a 2" foam brush, quickly coat the back of the recipe with decoupage medium and smooth it into position inside the penciled outline.

12. Use a burnishing tool to smooth out air pockets and excess decoupage medium, starting from the center of the recipe and working outward. Wipe away any excess medium with a damp paper towel. Let dry. To fix any remaining air pockets, use a craft knife to slit the paper, slide decoupage medium under the paper, then press pocket down. Brush entire recipe and table surface with several even coats of decoupage medium for protection. The finish will be water-resistant when dry.

SHOPPING LIST

- Kitchen table (square or rectangular shapes work best)
- Flat latex paint in seafoam green
- White butcher paper
- Computer and printer
- Spray-mount adhesive
- Yardstick ruler
- Craft knife
- Colored pencils
- Floral spray paint in glossy wood tone
- ¼" and ½" painters tape
- Acrylic craft paint in red
- ½" and 2" foam brushes
- Decoupage medium
- Burnishing tool
- Paper towels

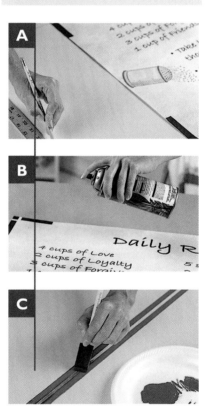

FUN AND FRUITY

FOR ANOTHER TAKE on this table, start with the same base color and decoupage it with cutouts from fruit-themed and pinstripe wallpaper. Use a rectangle of fruit-print paper in the center and border it with strips cut from green-and-white pinstripe paper. Cut an assortment of branch and fruit motifs from the fruit paper and use those to surround the center and fill out the edges of the table. To complete the look, decoupage fruit motifs to the fronts and backs of the dining chairs.

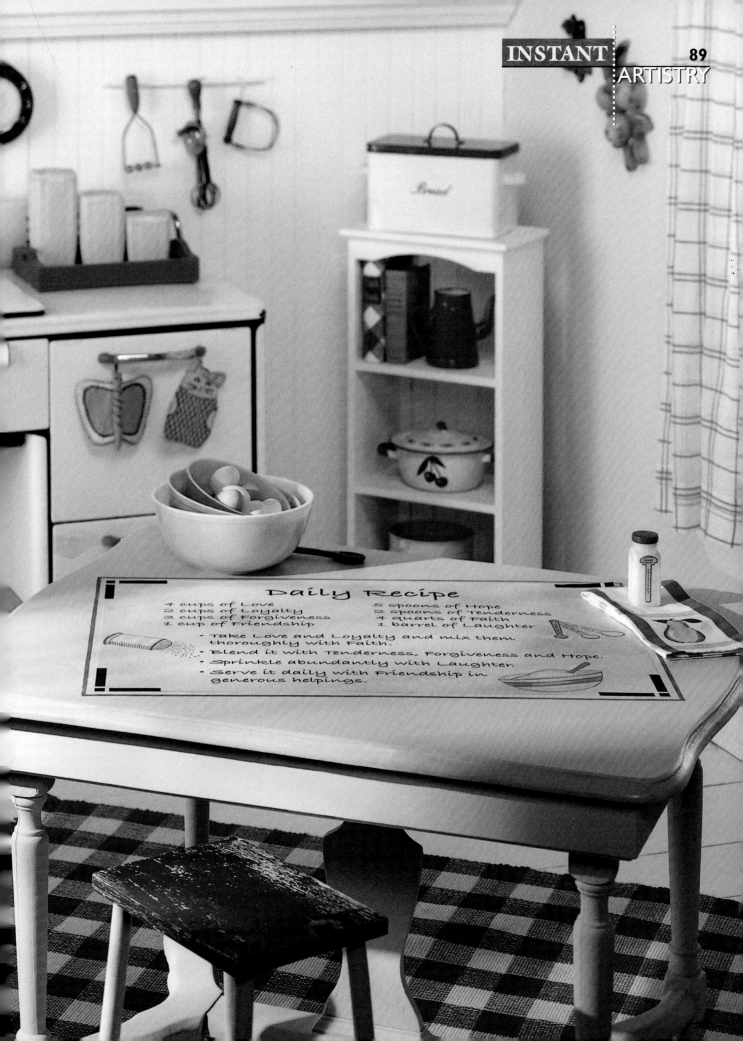

Daily Recipe

4 cups of Love
2 cups of Loyalty
3 cups of Forgiveness
1 cup of Friendship

5 spoons of Hope
2 spoons of Tenderness
4 quarts of Faith
1 barrel of Laughter

- Take Love and Loyalty and mix them thoroughly with Faith.
- Blend it with Tenderness, Forgiveness and Hope.
- Sprinkle abundantly with Laughter.
- Serve it daily with Friendship in generous helpings.

SUNFLOWER *Seat*

1. Sand chair and wipe with tack cloth. (Chair must be unfinished; finishes can burn and emit fumes during heat transfer.)

2. Determine the size and number of flowers to be transferred onto the chair back. To help plan your design, make plain photocopies. (The image will face the opposite direction after transferring, so make sure that you take this into consideration when planning your design. Photocopy your art in mirror image to visualize the finished design.) Cut around the images and tape the copies to the back of the chair, moving them around until you are satisfied with the placement. We used three evenly spaced sunflower images across our chair back.

3. Mark flower placement on chair and remove copies.

4. Make color photocopies of the flower image in the size, number and orientation determined above. Make extra copies for practice and in case you make mistakes.

5. Tape each copy in place on the chair back, aligning it with placement marks.

6. Press the tip of the heat or iron tool firmly against the surface, rubbing continuously in a circular motion on the back of the photocopy (see photo A). The heat will release the ink from the surface of the color copy and cause it to adhere to the wood. (This technique also works on fabric, paper and other porous surfaces, as well as ceramic and glass.)

7. Lift edge of the paper often to make sure the image is transferring properly (see photo B).

8. Remove paper completely after entire image has been transferred.

9. If any mistakes occur, use sandpaper to sand off areas that don't look right, or even the entire image, and start over with a fresh photocopy.

10. Seal the entire piece with a satin sealer.

SHOPPING LIST
- Unfinished wood chair with large back
- 300-grit sandpaper
- Tack cloth
- Copyright-free sunflower images
- Heat tool or iron
- Painters tape
- Color copier
- Scissors
- Clear satin sealer

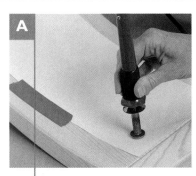

TIP: *To save transfer paper, you can create a single sheet with all three flowers on it. We scanned our floral image into our computer and printed out a page with three sunflowers on it, then had that copied onto the transfer paper.*

NATURE'S *Imprints*

1. Remove doors and drawers from cabinet and prepare for painting, applying primer, if needed.

2. When the primer is dry, paint the cabinet with flat white paint. Let dry.

3. Determine layout of leaves on cabinet. To add visual interest, tilt some of the leaves and overlap the edges. Because they are transparent, the overlapping leaves will create beautiful patterns. If a leaf is slightly too long, trim excess from the bottom following the natural veins that branch off the center stem. Remove matching sections from each half of the leaf.

4. When satisfied with the design, decoupage one leaf at a time. Hold the leaf in place and use the tip of a foam brush dipped in decoupage medium to gently pat the surface of leaf until it begins to bond to the cabinet (see photo A). Do not push hard; the leaves are fragile and can tear or lift away from the surface. Use your fingers to press down loose edges or work out wrinkles. Continue to apply remaining leaves to the surface.

5. Let dry completely, then apply a coat of decoupage medium over the entire leaf design. Let dry. Some portions of the leaves may wrinkle up with this second coat; gently press them down. Let dry.

6. Mix one part taupe paint with two parts glaze base in a plastic container. Use a ½" flat artist brush to apply glaze to highlight the edges of the drawers and doors (see photo B). Lightly wipe away excess glaze with a clean rag.

7. Seal entire piece with two to four coats of sealer.

8. Attach coordinating leaf knobs as an accent, if desired.

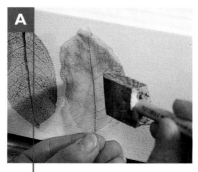

LEAFY ALTERNATIVES
- **USE PRESSED FLOWERS** or other plant material. Make sure the items are thoroughly dried and pressed flat or the technique will not work. You may need to use only the petals from a flower unless its center is very thin and flat, like a pansy.
- **IF YOU FIND THE REAL THING** too difficult to locate or work with, make color photocopies of silk leaves or blooms or of closeup photographs of leaves or flowers. Then carefully cut out the images and adhere as you would traditional paper decoupage.

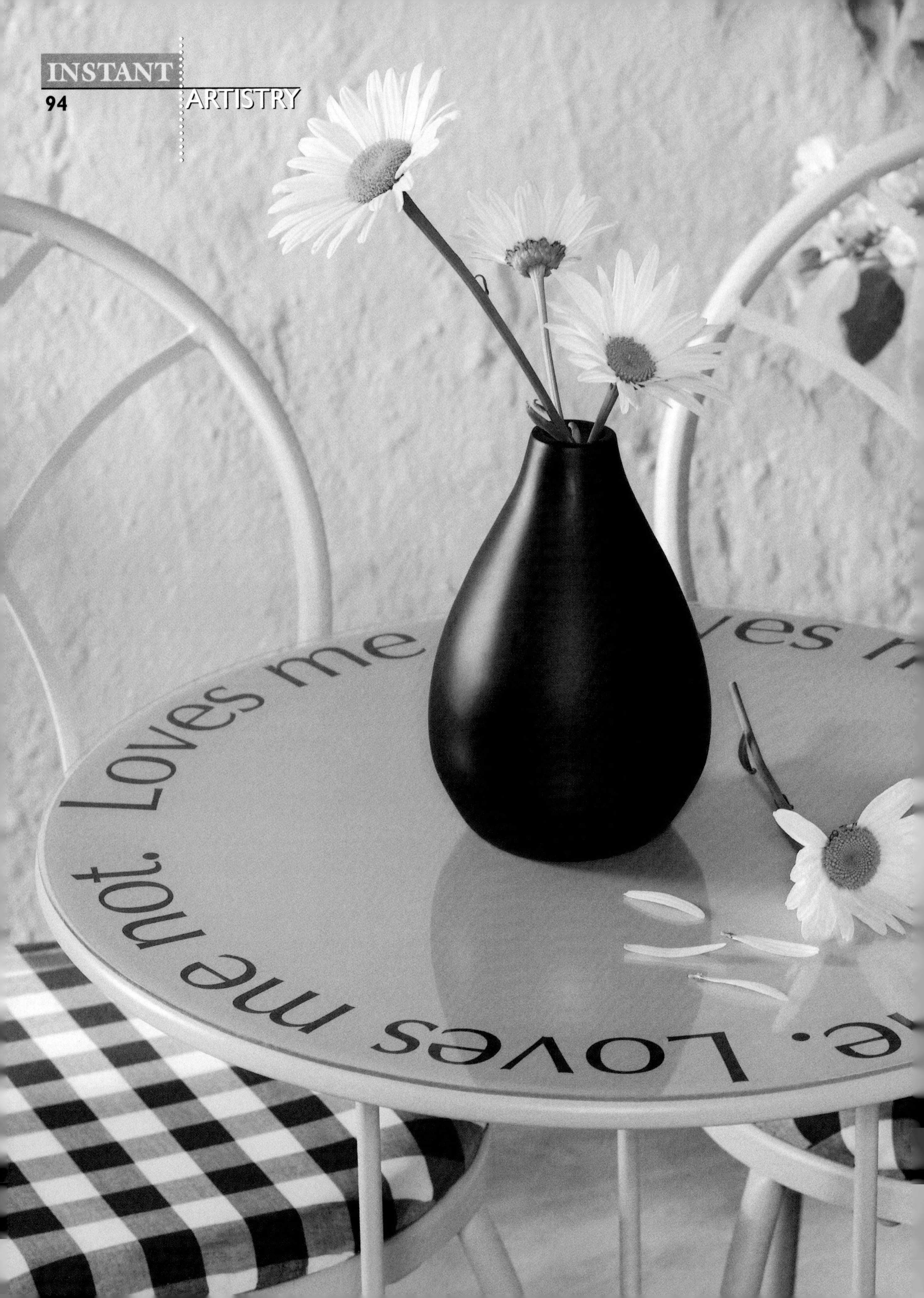
Loves me
ves m
Loves me not.
e. Loves

WORDS OF *Love*

1. Paint table desired color. (We painted our metal table with peppermint pink spray paint for metal surfaces.)

2. Create your own saying on a computer and enlarge it to fit your table. When creating your text, use desktop publishing software that allows you to curve words so they fit around the tabletop's perimeter.

3. Make a complete pattern by enlarging the phrase in sections and taping sheets of copy paper together, or cut apart the words and use them as a guide to plan design. If you're using our pattern, you may need to resize the words and adjust the curve to fit the size of your tabletop. Once you're satisfied with word size and curve, tape pieces together to secure arrangement. Using a pencil, mark along table edge to indicate where you'll place transfers.

4. Color photocopy the final layout onto image transfer paper, splitting words into sections to fit on sheets of transfer paper. (We were able to fit "Loves me" and "Loves me not" on one sheet of transfer paper.) Cut out each portion of the phrase from the transfer paper (see photo A).

5. Place the cutout phrase in a water-filled pan, and let it soak for a few minutes (see photo B). The backing will slowly begin to separate from the transfer. Be careful not to tear the transfer, as it is very delicate at this stage. (You may want to make extra copies in case you accidentally rip the transfer.) Lift the transfer from the water, discard the backing, and lay transfer onto table following previously marked guidelines.

6. Use your fingertips to slide the transfer into place. Press out any air bubbles, and then smooth with a burnishing tool to secure transfer to table. If you need to move the transfer, rewet it and slide it into the new position; transfers will not be completely secure until fully dry. Affix the second part of the phrase in the same manner as above and repeat for the entire tabletop. Let dry 24 hours.

7. Apply sealer to protect transfers.

TIP: *Transfers are still susceptible to wear after a coat of sealer; have a glass specialty shop cut a piece of glass to fit the tabletop to further protect the finish. To keep the glass from shifting around, you can place clear vinyl surface protectors beneath it.*

SHOPPING LIST

- Small round bistro table
- Peppermint pink spray paint
- Computer with desktop publishing software
- White copy paper
- Tape
- Image transfer paper for color photocopies
- Scissors
- Pan filled with water
- Burnishing tool
- Clear acrylic spray sealer

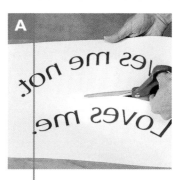

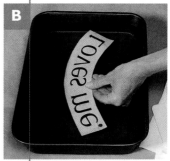

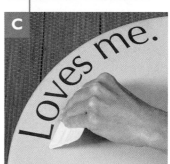

PAINTERLY
Images

CREATE A FUNCTIONAL WORK of art by applying a large-scale transfer to the front of a chest of drawers. Prepare the surface for painting and base-coat with white paint. We used a large transfer for the top four sections of our dresser; if your transfer is similar, preplan and measure the drawer fronts carefully before starting the transfer process. There may be slight differences in the sizes of the transfer image sheets; measure all transfers first and plan for differences, including calculating gaps between drawers. Double-check measurements before cutting. Cut transfer sheets into sections to fit drawer fronts, piecing them together when necessary. Using a sponge brush, apply a clear-coat sealer to furniture piece and let dry. Apply additional coats, if needed, to create a smooth, well-sealed surface. Apply imprint adhesive coat and the transfer following manufacturer's instructions (for more on this technique, see the instructions for the Butterfly Chair on page 84.)

After applying the transfers, apply a coat of sealer to protect the finish and neutralize the imprint adhesive coat. For the bottom drawer, we photocopied a favorite quotation in the style of the artwork, allowing space for the drawer pulls. If the quote is in sections, adhere together with decoupage medium. When dry, tear away excess paper around words to create an interesting shape. Adhere quote to cabinet with decoupage medium. Let dry. Lightly mist non-transfer areas of the cabinet with brown spray paint for an aged effect. Create speckles by partially depressing the nozzle to cause heavier drops of spray. Coat the quote with decoupage medium and let dry, then seal the entire dresser.

FLORAL *Photocopies*

MAKE COLOR COPIES of a favorite image and transfer them to a painted surface (smooth, eggshell finishes work best) with a heat tool. The process creates a weathered look. Select an image to be transferred, preferably in midtone or deeper colors because the image transfer process lightens colors. (Before making the color copies needed for the transfer process, make black-and-white copies in various sizes and arrange them on the furniture piece to determine size and design placement.) At a copy center, reproduce images in color, enlarging, if necessary. Make extra copies for placement and in case of error. We enlarged images to fit our piece and made mirror-image copies to create a balanced design. After determining placement and marking accordingly on furniture, turn the color copy facedown on the surface and tape the top of the paper in place. (Taping only the top allows you to lift the paper during the process to check your results.) Rub a heat tool (see Sunflower Seat, page 90, for more on this technique) across the back of the color copy. Continue until the entire image has transferred to the furniture surface. Remove the tape and discard the paper. Repeat the process to transfer remaining images. Coat the piece with clear matte sealer.

TERRIFIC TOILE

CREATE A TOILE LOOK on a piece of furniture using copyright-free images and image transfer paper. We used this treatment on a media cabinet with a distressed black and white finish. Photocopy and enlarge images or portions of images, then create a design to fit your furniture. Cut copies apart as needed and tape together, using whole and partial images to create a balanced design. If you're using portions of images, make sure to enlarge them at similar percentages. Tape the pieces to the cabinet to check the effect. When satisfied, transfer the dimensions of the area to be decorated to a large sheet of white paper. With pencil, mark horizontal and vertical centerlines and knob placement. Make new photocopies at the correct sizes and use them to recreate the artwork for each area, using a glue stick to paste sections together to form the final image. Trim and overlap to hide areas where sections join. (You can also add line art here or fill in with a fine-point black permanent marker.) Take paste-ups to copy store and have them copied in reverse on image transfer paper for photocopies. (Depending on size, you may have to copy in sections and rejoin the pieces during the transfer process.) Because transfers are delicate, make several copies in case of error during application. On your furniture piece, mark vertical and horizontal center points on the edges of each design area for placement guide. Wipe area with damp sponge. Follow paper manufacturer's instructions for wetting transfer. Position transfer facedown on surface and slide paper backing away. Take care to hide any joints between sections. Do not overlap; trim any excess with craft knife or scissors. Smooth out any bubbles with your fingers. Apply remaining transfers in the same manner. Let dry. Apply clear acrylic spray sealer.

BEFORE

IN Tune

DECOUPAGED SHEET MUSIC and an antique finish hit a high note on this boxy storage cabinet. Paint the cabinet with camel paint and let dry. Dry brush antique white paint on top of the camel paint. Let dry. Make photocopies of sheet music to fit the width of each door panel, leaving approximately 1 inch all around for a border. You may need to use more than one sheet of music to fit the length of your panel area; just trim the excess and overlap edges slightly to fill the space. Use decoupage medium to glue the sheet music in place on the center of each door panel (see page 88, Steps 11 and 12, for detailed instructions on applying decoupage medium). Continue until all sheets are in place on the cabinet. Let dry. Using a foam brush, seal panel area with a coat of decoupage medium. Mix one part light brown acrylic craft paint with two parts glaze base. Apply the mixture over the sheet music with a 2" paintbrush (see photo). Wipe off excess with a soft, slightly damp cloth. Protect the finish with two coats of matte sealer. Let dry. Attach decorative knobs.

DAISY DELIGHT

GIVE AN OLD TABLE A CHEERY, flower-strewn look with bright paint and gift-wrap cutouts. Paint the table with green paint. Let dry. Measure and tape off a square area in the center of the tabletop and paint yellow. Remove tape and let dry. Cut floral images from wrapping paper and determine placement on the tabletop, marking lightly with pencil. We placed cutouts around the edge of the table, overlapping a few onto the center square. After you have determined the arrangement, use decoupage medium to glue the cutouts in place (see page 88, Steps 11 and 12, for detailed instructions on applying decoupage medium). Continue until all cutouts are in place. Let dry. Using a wide paintbrush, seal the tabletop with a thin coat of decoupage medium.

A BOUQUET
of Blooms

ACHIEVE THIS COLLAGE LOOK by using a decoupage technique over a distressed paint treatment. Base-coat a chair with a sunny yellow paint (or a color that coordinates with your room). Let dry. Sand edges lightly and apply a golden-brown glaze for an aged look. Let dry. Enlarge a variety of rose images from a copyright-free publication to desired sizes and cut out the shapes. Select a range of colors. We used red, pink and peachy-yellow roses on our yellow chair. Arrange cutouts onto the chair seat until you have a pleasing design. We used enough rose cutouts to cover most of the seat. After you have determined the arrangement, use decoupage medium to glue the cutouts in place (see page 88, Steps 11 and 12, for detailed instructions on applying decoupage medium). Seal the surface with a coat of decoupage medium. Use a single cutout to accent the chair back. To complete the look, use a small leaf stamp to stamp around the chair back motif and around the edge of the chair seat.

CREATIVE

Conversions

102

106

108

110

SOMETIMES FURNISHINGS seem to have outlived their usefulness, such as pieces that are damaged or missing parts or those that are hopelessly outdated. In these cases, you need more than fresh finish, you need a fresh outlook. Try "repurposing"—turning items into brand-new pieces that serve different functions than those for which they were designed, such as making a chair into a table or a dresser into a bar cart. On the flip side, you can also turn non-furniture items, like pallets, shutters and birdbaths, into one-of-a-kind creations.

MIRROR *Table*

1. Choose two old table legs large enough to support your arched window. The window's curved edge will become the front of the wall-mounted table, while the flat side will rest against the wall, supported by L brackets.

2. Evenly space legs along the curved part of the window frame and attach with L brackets and screws. (Choose brackets and supports suited to your window.)

3. Tape off or cover window glass with paper. Dry brush entire piece with golden tan paint. Let dry.

4. Dry brush balustrade with golden tan paint. Let dry.

5. Plan mirror placement on back of balustrade. Have a mirror cut to fit the area selected. (Our section of balustrade was missing several balusters, which allowed for a mirror opening. If you find a section of balustrade that is intact, remove some of the balusters.)

6. Attach mirror to back of balustrade, using mirror clips and 1¼" screws (see photo A).

7. Plan placement of the window table on the wall. Lightly pencil a level guideline where the bottom edge of the window frame meets the wall for L bracket placement.

8. Space three L brackets evenly along the marked guideline and attach to the wall using drywall screws. (If possible, secure L brackets into wall studs or use medium-weight drywall anchors.)

9. Place window frame against wall, resting it on the L brackets (see photo B).

10. Center mirror above the table, with 4 inches between mirror and table. Using a yardstick level and pencil, mark a guideline for mirror L bracket placement. Remove table from brackets.

11. Attach two L brackets, evenly spaced on guideline, to support mirror.

12. Attach eye hooks on back of top rail at each end. Run picture wire through eye hooks, wrapping wire around itself to secure before trimming with wire cutters.

13. Attach picture hook to wall. Place balustrade mirror on L brackets and picture wire over hook. Using two 1¼" drywall screws, attach base of balustrade to L brackets.

14. Set window table on brackets and secure by driving drywall screws up through brackets into window frame. (If there is a gap between the wall and tabletop, fill in with a piece of wood trim.)

SHOPPING LIST

- Arched window
- Two furniture legs (ours were salvaged from an old dining table)
- L brackets
- Flat latex paint in golden tan
- Paintbrushes
- Portion of old balustrade
- Mirror (cut to fit within balustrade)
- Four mirror clips with 1¼" screws
- 1¼" drywall screws
- Three medium-weight drywall anchors or molly bolts
- Drill
- Yardstick level
- Two eye hooks
- Heavy-gauge picture wire
- Wire cutters
- Heavyweight picture hook

TYING IT TOGETHER ....

WE WERE LUCKY enough to find parts that all had a similar white, chippy finish, which we tied together by dry brushing lightly with golden tan paint for an antique look. You may find an assortment of pieces with just the right shape, but in a mishmash of finishes or colors. In that case, paint them all the same color, such as white or black, then distress the edges or antique with dry brushing for a unified look.

DRESSER
a la Carte

1. Remove the top two drawers from the dresser. Base-coat the interior of the dresser with maple latex paint. Let dry. (Our dresser has shelves built in between each drawer. If your dresser doesn't have these shelves, cut a piece of plywood or sturdy paneling to fit atop the drawer rails.)

2. Remove handles from drawers.

3. Base-coat exterior of dresser (including the drawer fronts) with antique white paint. Let dry.

4. Measure the sides of the dresser top and use a hacksaw to cut metal towel bars to each measurement to fit around the top of the dresser as a rail.

5. Lightly sand towel bars, bathrobe hooks and new drawer pulls and spray them with metal primer. Let dry. Base-coat with copper spray paint (see photo A).

6. While the base coat is still tacky, give towel bars an aged and tarnished look with flecks of paint. To do this, hold down the spray nozzle halfway as you lightly spritz the bars with dark brown, terra-cotta and cherry wood tone floral spray paint.

7. Apply a coat of spray sealer to the bars to seal the surface. Let dry.

8. To simulate the aged appearance shown on the front of the dresser, mix one part burnt umber acrylic paint with three parts glaze in a plastic container. Lightly wipe the glaze mixture onto the drawers with a rag. Use a spray bottle to mist the surface with water, giving it a mottled appearance.

9. Repeat Step 8, using a small amount of black acrylic paint and glaze. Let dry.

10. Fasten pulls to the drawers and bars to the top of the dresser. Replace dresser's legs with casters (see photo B).

BEFORE

A

B

EASY ENTERTAINING

THIS ROLLING BAR CART features hooks on the side to hold towels, drawer storage for linens and silverware and open storage for glasses. A top rail keeps bottles and snacks secure when you're moving the cart. In the open storage area, place non-skid shelf liner to keep glasses from shifting. Use old soda bottle crates and wicker baskets to stow cocktail garnishes and accessories out of sight.

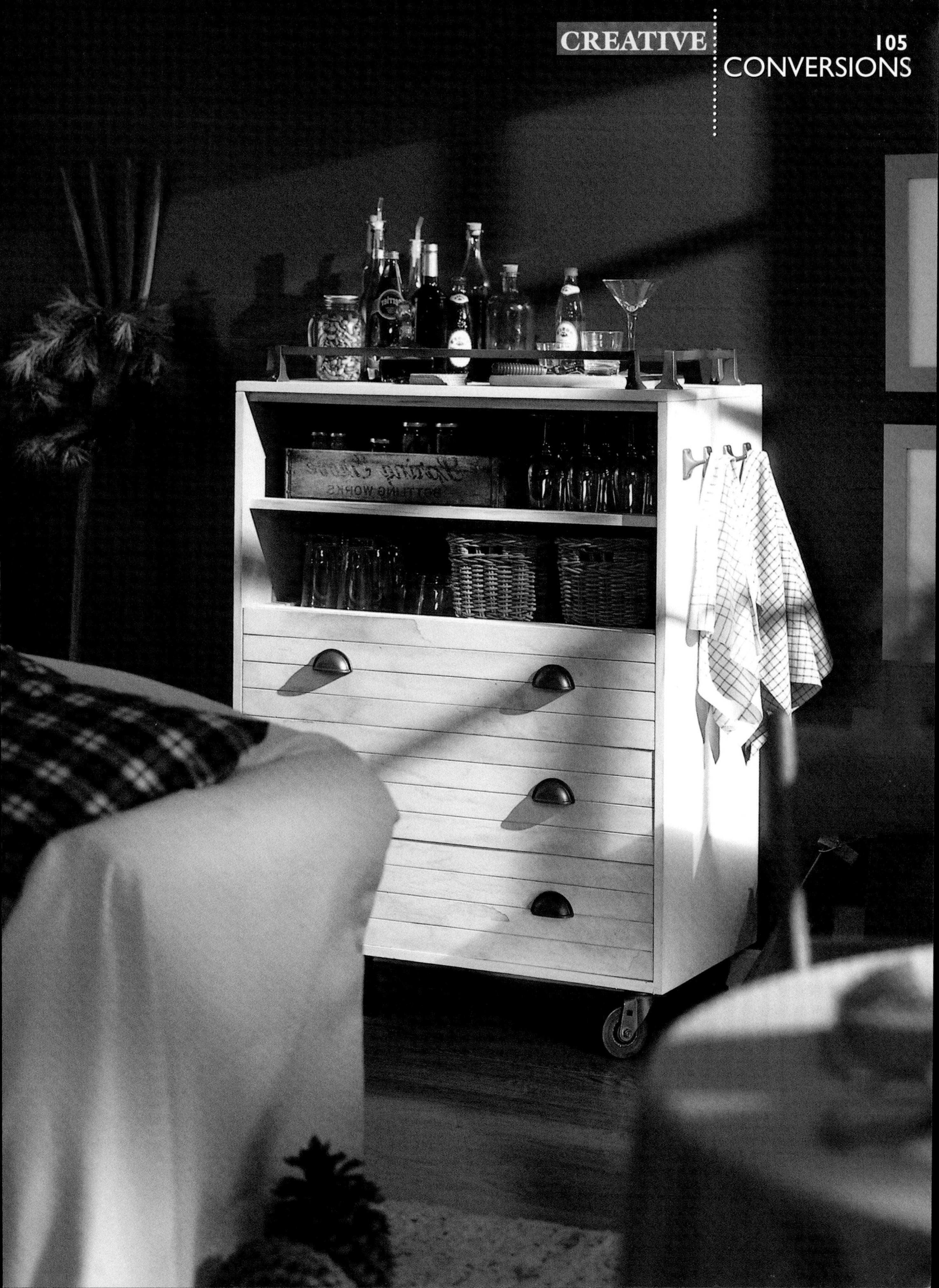

DISTRESS AND DECOUPAGE

PREPARE CABINET AND FRAMES for painting. Base-coat entire cabinet and half of the frames with celery green paint. Base-coat remaining frames with antique white paint. Let dry overnight. Use a candle-wax resist technique (for more on this, see page 122). Rub candle liberally over select areas of the cabinet and frames, then top-coat cabinet with antique white and frames with either antique white or celery, depending on base color. Let dry. Sand waxed areas and wipe with a tack cloth. Decoupage botanical fruit images onto the outer panel of the cabinet. With a sponge brush, apply decoupage medium to the back of the motif, center, then smooth into place using a burnishing tool. Seal cabinet and frames with satin-finish sealer. Let dry.

JUMBO *Jewelry Box*

BEFORE

SHOPPING LIST

- Cabinet
- ½" plywood
- Circular saw
- Assorted frames
- Quarter-round molding
- T square
- Pencil
- Miter box and backsaw
- Drill, bits and countersink bit
- Power screwdriver
- ¾" and 2½" screws
- 2" trim molding
- Brad nails
- Wood putty
- Pine table legs
- Construction adhesive
- Foam brush
- Flat latex paint in celery green and antique white
- White wax candle
- Botanical image for decoupage
- Decoupage medium
- Burnishing tool
- Satin-finish sealer
- Foamboard
- Sheet or tile cork
- Spray-mount adhesive
- Fleece fabric
- Two coordinating green cotton print fabrics
- Scissors
- Small decorative knobs
- White glue
- Mat board
- Epoxy

1. Remove existing shelving or dividers from inside cabinet. Make needed repairs to the cabinet and replace any warped or weak parts.

2. Picture frames act as drawers to hold jewelry. To hold them in place, you need to add preassembled side rail inserts made from pieces of quarter-round molding attached to plywood and placed inside the cabinet. Cut two ½" plywood panels to the inside dimensions of the cabinet sides. (This will make the width of the cabinet interior about 1 inch narrower; plan accordingly when purchasing frames.)

3. Determine spacing of the side rails according to the depth and number of frames used. (The bottom frame does not need rails; it will rest on the cabinet bottom.) On each plywood piece, indicate the top and bottom and mark corresponding parallel guidelines ½ inch apart on each board for side rail placement using a pencil and a T square (see photo A). Transfer measurements to the second board.

4. Using a miter box and backsaw, cut lengths of quarter round to fit boards for side rails.

5. Predrill three holes on the marked side of the plywood boards for each rail placement. Evenly space the holes and center them between the guidelines. From the back side of the board, countersink each hole and drive ¾" screws through the predrilled holes so that just the tips show on the marked side of the board. Align rails over guidelines and screw tips. Use a power screwdriver to attach rails to the board (see photo B).

6. Slide assembled boards into the cabinet. Attach the boards from the inside to the cabinet frame using ¾" screws, predrilling and countersinking the heads.

7. For a finished look, cover the areas where the plywood boards meet the cabinet face of with 2"-wide trim. Use a miter box and backsaw to cut trim to fit and attach with brad nails. Countersink nail heads and fill holes with wood putty.

8. Determine placement of legs on underside of cabinet, measuring and marking for even placement. Attach with construction adhesive and three 2½" screws driven through the base of the cabinet into the leg. Countersink screws and fill holes with wood putty.

9. Use a distressing technique to finish the cabinet and frames (see box).

10. Create fabric-covered panels to insert into the frame openings using foamboard. Cut the foamboard pieces ¼" smaller than the length and width dimensions of each frame. (If pieces do not fit snugly into the opening, attach a layer of cork to boards with spray mount.)

11. Cut fleece to the dimensions of the foamboard inserts and attach with spray mount.

12. Select two coordinating fabrics and use them on alternating frames. Cut fabric pieces large enough to wrap over to the back side of the padded boards. Attach with white glue, pulling fabric tightly over edges and trimming excess at corners, if needed. Set assembly facedown on a flat surface, weight and let dry overnight.

13. Cut mat board to cover the entire back of the frame. Cut fabric to fit over the mat board, with 2" extra on all sides, and glue as above. Glue covered mat board to frame back and add clamps or weight. Let dry overnight.

14. Insert finished frame drawers into cabinet. Add knobs to the frames to act as drawer pulls. Drill holes and use epoxy to secure in place. Let dry.

A

B

BEFORE

1. Select one or more shutters to use for your hall tree based on the amount of space available. (For aesthetics, we planned for the wider part of the shutter frames to be at the top, allowing for hook placement.) Place the shutters side by side, facedown, and secure together with four evenly spaced 4" mending plates (see photo A).

2. Stand shutters up in the desired corner. Shutters will be braced at the top and bottom against triangular support pieces of ½" plywood cut to fit into the corner. For the sides of the top support triangle, measure from the front edge of the shutters into the corner along the wall. Add 1 inch to this measurement so the front edge of the plywood will overhang the shutters. Because the support is a right triangle, the length of the front edge will be determined by the length of the sides. The bottom support fits behind the shutters. For the sides of the bottom piece, measure along the wall from the back edge of the shutters into the corner, just above the molding. Transfer the measurements for the top and bottom supports to separate corners of a sheet of plywood. Cut out with a jigsaw. Paint the supports white on both sides to match the shutter color.

3. Attach two 2" L brackets upright on the surface along each side of the bottom support, evenly spaced and aligned with the edges. Attach the bottom support to the wall with screws, placing it flush into the corner.

4. Determine the height at which the top support will be attached to the wall. Measure from the floor to the top edge of your shutters. Mark placement for top support on wall with pencil. Attach two 2" L brackets upright on the surface along each side of the top support, evenly spaced and aligned with the edges. Position the support with the brackets on the underside and the bottom edge aligned with marked guidelines. Attach the brackets to the wall with screws (see photo B).

5. Slide the shutter unit into position in the corner. The bottom of the unit should be pushed tightly against the front edge of the bottom support. The top edge of the unit should have the support extending 1 inch past it. With pencil, mark a horizontal line on the back of the shutter frames where it rests against the bottom support. On the frame, mark points along the line for screw placement and drill pilot holes at these points. Set shutter unit in place and drive screws through holes from the front of the shutters into the support. Secure the top support to the top edge of the shutter unit with four screws driven down from the top.

6. Determine shelf placement. Allow for the placement of a mirror centered above the shelf. Paint shelf white and mount it across the front of the shutter unit, driving screws into the outer frame edge of the shutter unit.

7. Add coat hooks to the top and outer frame of the shutter unit, where desired, with screws.

8. Hang the mirror in the upper portion of the shutter unit and attach with screws to the frames at the center.

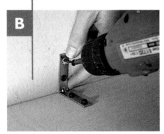

CLOSET OF YESTERYEAR

THE ENTRYWAYS OF TODAY are far from the grand foyers of the past, but the two share a common problem—a lack of storage. We used a pair of old shutters, plywood, a decorative shelf, hooks and a mirror to create a space-saving hall tree with the feel of those from the Victorian era. To round out the space, add a coordinating coatrack and umbrella stand.

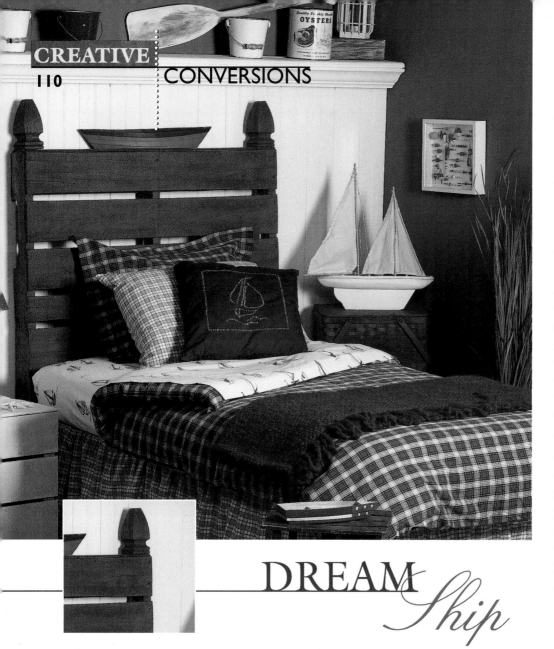

TURN A SIMPLE WOODEN SHIPPING PALLET into a first-class headboard. To locate a shipping pallet, ask a local business that receives freight deliveries if it has any extras. They are often discarded after use. Choose a pallet with square construction that has decent, even boards. Small imperfections will be hidden with a little paint, and you can renail any loose boards. To turn it into a headboard, set the pallet on its edge so the boards run horizontally. Cover the opening along the top by attaching a 4"-wide trim board with wood glue and screws. This also creates the upper edge of the headboard. At each top corner, about 2 inches in, predrill a hole, then attach a decorative fence-post finial. After the piece is assembled, paint it to suit your decor (we used red) and let dry. To highlight the texture and grain of the wood, lightly dry brush a brighter shade of acrylic paint over the base coat.

DREAM *Ship*

SHUTTER SOFA TABLE

SPLASH A BIT OF BRIGHT COLOR into your living room with this shutter sofa table. Start with three pairs of shutters. (The two pairs to be used on each end must be the same height; the center pair can be shorter since it is not needed for support.) Paint shutters desired colors. We painted ours in an array of country hues. To make the base, hinge together two shutters to make each pair. Set the taller hinged shutter pairs in V shapes to make them freestanding. Set the smaller pair of shutters between the others for design interest. Place a piece of tempered glass on top of the shutters. Add vinyl surface protectors between the shutters and glass to keep glass from shifting.

A FEW EASY MODIFICATIONS transform a common wooden stepladder into a CD storage unit. Create support bars for CDs to rest against. We chose to place support bars 3 inches above each step so that CDs could be turned vertically or horizontally. If you would like to use this for videotapes or DVDs, you will need to adjust placement of the support bars to suit the size of the items. For each bar, measure up 3 inches from the step and measure the distance across the front of the stepladder at that point. Cut a piece of ¾" x 2½" pine trim to each measurement. Use screws to attach 2" L brackets to the back of each support bar, with the L bracket extending around the end. Align the support bar 3 inches above the middle step on the back side of the ladder and attach with screws through the L bracket to the outside edge of the ladder. Make sure the board is level and parallel to the step. Repeat to attach support bar for the lower step. Apply one or two coats of beige paint to the stepladder. Let dry. To make the piece into an end table, center a 16-inch round tabletop on top of the stepladder, positioning round protective vinyl pads evenly between the glass and edge of the stepladder to keep the glass from slipping. Place CDs on the steps, resting them against the supports.

MUSICAL *Stairs*

NOT JUST
for the Birds

USE A PAIR OF DECORATIVE BIRDBATHS to make a base for a glass-topped table. We started with two 18"-diameter birdbaths with a diamond pattern and had a rectangular piece of glass custom cut for the tabletop. Inspired by the design on the birdbaths, we cut a triangle-shaped stamp from expandable sponge to use on the tabletop edge. We also cut a small square from the sponge for the table corners. Expand sponge shapes in water. Clean glass and prepare for glass paint following manufacturer's instructions. (Be careful not to touch the glass; oil from hands can interfere with paint bond.) Slide a quilters ruler under the glass, aligning the ½-inch guideline with the bottom edge of the glass (see photo). The inch marks serve as a guide for placing triangles. Press triangle stamp into white glass paint. Starting 3 inches from the outside edge of the glass, align the point and centerline of the stamp with the 3-inch mark and press in place. Use more pressure on the triangle tip and less on the base. Continue around tabletop edge, leaving space at corners for squares. Stamp a white square at each corner, aligning it with triangle bases. Let dry. Set up birdbaths with tops about 6 inches apart. Fill birdbaths with desired materials, such as shells, stones, dried leaves or moss. Place clear vinyl surface protectors around edges to protect and lift glass. Center glass, paint side down, over birdbaths.

BEDSIDE CHARMER

AN OLD WICKER CHAIR with an ornate back makes a fanciful bedside table. Spray paint an old chair white. Measure the diameter of the chair seat and have a round piece of glass cut to fit. Hang the chair from the wall next to a bed. (The chair is not meant to hold very heavy objects.) Depending on the structure and weight of your chair, determine how to best hang it. Hold the chair up to the wall to see what portion will rest against the wall. Use screws, hooks or L brackets to secure the chair in place. Use clear vinyl surface protectors between the glass and chair seat or secure the glass to the wicker with clear silicone and let dry.

DOOR *Headboard*

HANG AN OLD DOOR on the wall to act as a headboard. Orient the door sideways to find and mark the vertical centerline. Measure width of bed and mark the vertical centerline on the wall above the bed. (We hung our weathered door as we found it, with hardware attached. If you are using a door that has loose or chipping paint, apply sealer to prevent the paint from flaking off.) Locate wall studs over bed. (These may not be aligned with bed placement.) Using a level, mark the stud locations with pencil. Lean the door against the wall and line up premarked centerlines of door with wall and mark stud placement on edge of door. This will determine where your mounting pieces need to be attached. Because of the weight and size of most doors and to mount the door so it hangs flush against the wall, we recommend using professional flush-mounted hanger/fasteners secured into the wall studs with #6 x 2" wood screws. Instead, you could attach large hitching rings to the door and heavy-duty hooks to the walls at stud locations.) Follow the kit instructions to attach the hanger/fasteners to the door and wall. Have a friend help you lift the door and interlock the hangers and holder. Add framed botanical prints to the headboard to create a pretty display.

DOUBLE STACK

EXTEND AN OLD NIGHTSTAND'S FUNCTION with the addition of a tabletop and legs. The new table not only supplies a dining surface, but also offers storage. Purchase four coffee-table legs and a round tabletop from a home center. If needed, cut down the nightstand legs and the table legs or replace the nightstand legs with shorter ones to achieve the desired height. Determine and mark placement of second set of legs on each corner of the nightstand top and predrill holes at marked points. (Hold drill as straight as possible for proper leg alignment.) Add second set of legs using a kit that includes metal dowel screws and dowel driver. Twist legs in place. Make a tabletop support from a piece of 3/4" plywood cut to the size of the nightstand top. Place the plywood piece on top of the second set of legs and drive 2" screws through plywood and into each leg. To attach the tabletop to the plywood base, predrill holes, placing at least one between each set of legs. Center the tabletop over the plywood. Drive screws from the underside through the predrilled holes into the tabletop. Paint the entire piece. Let dry. Protect the finish with a coat of clear sealer.

AGING *Gracefully*

HASTEN THE PASSAGE OF TIME
with treatments that give newer pieces
antique appeal. Use crackle medium to
replicate an aging finish, employ everyday
tools to lend distressed character, or try
resist techniques to suggest built-up layers
of paint—and watch your furniture grow
old before your eyes!

DISTRESSED *Wall Cabinet*

1. Paint the piece in your choice of color. We used warm white. (This technique can also be done on an unpainted piece, but the effect is more pronounced on a painted surface.)

2. Use an awl to poke many holes into the surface, grouping them in heavy, random clusters (see photo A). Group clusters to create various sizes and shapes. For a more natural look, make the clusters heavier at the center and thinner at the edges. (Balance is important; if you have a heavy spot on one side of the piece, you may need to add another heavy cluster or a group of several small clusters on the opposite corner.)

3. Use the awl to poke single holes scattered over the entire surface of the cabinet or in small groupings of three to five holes.

4. Use a utility knife to slice through the centers of the larger clusters. Slice following the wood grain over

and over again (see photo B). Slightly angle the blade to loosen large slivers of wood. The wood in the awl-damaged areas will break loose and chip out easily. If you like, go back and poke the slivered areas with the awl to create deeper indentations.

5. Use a wire brush to further distress the surface, especially the hole clusters, again following the wood grain (see photo C). The wire brush will quickly abrade the exposed wood, creating natural-looking gouged channels, and will remove patches of paint around the distressed areas.

6. Finish by applying brown glaze to the entire piece (see photo D). The awl-gouged areas will absorb a lot of glaze because of the exposed grain, so apply extra glaze to these areas. (You can use a darker stain to further highlight the damage.)

7. Protect the finish with a coat of clear matte sealer.

SHOPPING LIST

- Wall cabinet or other furniture piece
- Flat latex paint in warm white
- Awl
- Utility knife
- Wire brush
- Brown glaze
- Soft rags
- Clear matte sealer

MORE DISTRESSING TOOLS

ROCK—Use a sharp-edged, palm-sized rock to beat a painted or unpainted surface randomly, changing position to create different types of indentations. Scrape pointed edges across the surface to make interesting gouges. Highlight distressing with stain or glaze.

NAIL SET—Use a nail set with a small point to produce the look of wood pitted with the tracks of burrowing worms. This technique works best on soft, unpainted wood. Hold the handle in your palm and press gently into wood, moving the tool forward to create a line about ½ inch long. Create main tracks following the wood grain, then add branches and short disconnected tracks. Apply a stain or glaze to showcase the tracks.

CHISEL—Use a small, sharp chisel on unpainted wood to chip and gouge pieces from the surface. Hold the tool in line with the grain and push the tip in until it catches under the grain. Pull up the loose piece. (For hardwoods, you may need to tap the chisel end with a hammer. Wear goggles and work away from your body.) Smooth ragged edges with sandpaper and finish with a stain.

CRACKLED *Chest*

1. Apply two coats of primer to the chest. Let dry.

2. Paint entire chest with gold paint. Let dry.

3. Determine size of stripes and mark placement on drawer fronts using a straightedge. (The drawers on our chest were 30 inches wide. Because we decided to use 3-inch stripes, we marked the placement of the first stripe 1½ inches in from the side edge of the drawer and continued across the piece measuring and marking 3-inch stripes. This resulted in nine 3-inch stripes in the center of the drawer front and a 1½-inch stripe on each end.) Experiment with stripe width, making them thicker or thinner to suit your piece, or change the orientation from vertical to horizontal.

4. Mask off alternating stripes with painters tape and use a foam brush to paint with ivory paint (see photo A). Let dry.

5. Using a stiff-bristled paintbrush, apply crackle medium to the ivory stripes (see photo). Apply crackle medium more thickly in some areas to create varying textures. Let dry according to manufacturer's instructions.

6. Apply gold paint over the crackle medium using a sea sponge. Let dry. Brush sealer over the crackled stripes. Let dry overnight. Remove all tape.

7. Mask off the plain stripes with painters tape. Repeat Steps 5 and 6 for crackle and paint application, using ivory paint over crackle medium on the gold stripes. Remove tape. Let dry. Apply sealer to these stripes. Let dry.

8. For crackling and painting sides of chest, again follow steps 5 and 6 using ivory paint. Apply sealer. Let dry.

9. Cover all sides by taping sheets of kraft paper along the upper edge of the chest, underneath the top. Spray the top with silver metallic spray paint. Apply clear spray sealer. Remove paper and tape. Let dry.

10. Paint the drawer edges with silver acrylic craft paint. Let dry. Apply sealer. Let dry.

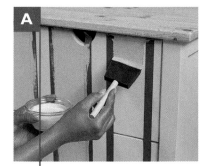

A

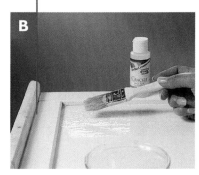

B

BEFORE

CRACKLE TIPS

- When applying the crackle, the direction of the brush strokes determines the primary direction of the crackle.
- The thicker the coat of crackle medium, the wider the cracks will be. Using a blow-dryer on the area will also create larger cracks.
- To achieve fine cracks, like the crazing found on old porcelain, lightly dab on crackle medium in a circular motion using a makeup sponge.
- Areas with a heavier coat of crackle medium will dry more slowly. Try not to go over the same area twice or you will reduce the number of cracks.

LIGHTLY *Dusted*

1. Lightly sand and prime piece with stain-blocking primer. Base-coat the piece with flat white latex paint (see photo A). Let dry. (When working with a piece of furniture that is upholstered, be sure to cover and tape off fabric areas and paint carefully.)

2. Mix one part light sage green paint with two parts glaze base on a foam plate. Paint the chair with the glaze mixture (see photo B).

3. While the paint is still tacky, apply the rottenstone by dipping a stencil brush into the rottenstone and patting it into the carvings and crevices of the chair (see photo C). (Practice application on a less-noticeable portion of the piece.) For a heavier application, reapply glaze mixture in the crevices of the furniture and apply more rottenstone on top of the glaze.

4. Wipe away any excess rottenstone dust with a clean rag (see photo D). Let dry overnight.

5. Protect the finish by brushing on clear matte sealer. Let dry.

6. If desired, re-upholster the chair with new fabric for a fresh look. We covered ours with a vintage floral print and coordinating trim.

SHOPPING LIST

- Old chair or other furniture piece with lots of carved detailing
- Sandpaper
- Kraft paper
- Painters tape
- Stain-blocking primer
- Flat latex paint in white and light sage green
- Paintbrushes
- Glaze base
- Foam plate
- Rottenstone
- Stencil brush
- Clean rag
- Clear matte sealer

A

B

C

D

BEFORE

AGING OPTIONS

ANOTHER WAY TO GIVE a piece with carved detailing the look of something that's spent years in Grandma's attic is to apply antiquing medium on top of a lighter finish. Simply wipe away excess, allowing the medium to settle in cracks and crevices. Or, try dry brushing over a lighter base coat with a gray or brown glaze, highlighting decorative areas on the piece.

WAXING *Nostalgic*

1. Decide which areas of the table you'd like to distress to plan placement of colors that will show through the top coat. (We distressed the edge of the tabletop and random spots on each leg to try and re-create the look of years of natural wear and tear on an old piece that has been repainted many colors.)

2. To make it look like there are several layers of color painted one on top of the other, brush small spots of each color except white randomly across the areas to be distressed later (see photo A). Let dry.

3. Rub a candle over the areas you wish to distress (see photo B).

4. Paint the table with white paint. Let dry.

5. Lightly sand the waxed spots with medium-grade sandpaper to reveal the colors underneath (see photo C).

6. Paint chairs white. Just like on the table, rub a wax candle over the areas of the chairs to be distressed.

7. Paint each chair with a different color, selecting from those used on the distressed table. Let dry.

8. Lightly sand the waxed spots with medium-grade sandpaper, allowing some of the original white base coat to show through. (We sanded some areas more heavily than others to uncover some of the natural wood of the chair for a more realistic look.)

9. Top-coat all pieces with one or two coats of a clear matte sealer, following manufacturer's instructions.

SHOPPING LIST

- Table and chairs
- Semigloss latex paint in white, lemon yellow, sky blue, light pink and lavender
- 1/2" paintbrush
- White wax candle
- Medium-grade sandpaper
- Clear matte sealer

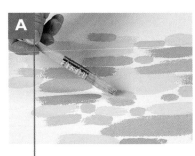

OTHER RESIST TECHNIQUES

RESIST TECHNIQUES help age furniture by making it easy to remove the top coat of paint from selected areas. You just need to apply a barrier medium to those areas where you wish to chip, peel or sand away paint. On our cottage table, we used candle wax, which produces a subtle, scratchy look, but you can also use paste wax, petroleum jelly or rubber cement. This cabinet (above left) combines rubber cement resist with sandpaper distressing, stenciling and a light crackle glaze. The resist technique was used on the cabinet top and on the beveled edge surrounding the door panel.

GIULIANA LAZZERINI ANCIENT HILL

GIVE A SIDE TABLE French country charm with scraps of toile wallpaper and a worn-looking finish. Remove hardware and prepare the piece for painting. Base-coat the table with two coats of white paint using a 3″ paintbrush. Let dry between coats. Apply a small amount of barn red acrylic craft paint to a foam brush and drag the brush lightly over some of the corners and edges of the piece to give the finish an aged look. Use light strokes so the paint appears faded. If you apply too much red, cover it with white paint. Next, measure the areas where you would like to apply wallpaper. (For our side table, we covered the door inset panel and the sides and back of the shelf area.) For each area, cut a piece 1 inch larger all around then your measurements. Working on one area at a time, apply decoupage medium to the surface that will be wallpapered and also to the back of the corresponding wallpaper piece. Smooth the piece in place and go over it with a burnishing tool to press out excess glue and air bubbles. Wipe off excess glue with a damp rag. Let dry. Use a craft knife to trim excess paper (see photo). To protect the paper and make it easier to keep clean, apply another layer of decoupage medium on top of it. Let dry. Replace hardware. (We added a decorative red glass knob to complement the colors and style of the finish.)

TIMEWORN *Toile*

TURN BACK THE CLOCK with a crackle treatment created with milk-based paints. Start with an unfinished piece for best results. (If your piece is finished, you'll need to use a special sealer in order for the treatment to work.) Make sure the surface is free of dirt and grease and wipe it down with a moist cloth. We used red milk paint for the base coat and mustard for the top coat. Mix paint for the base coat following the manufacturer's instructions. Apply a coat of red milk paint to the cabinet using a 2" foam brush. Let dry. Lightly sand over the first coat and wipe with a tack cloth, then apply a second coat of red paint. Let dry. Apply antique crackle medium in a generous, even coat using a bristle brush. Let dry following manufacturer's instructions. While the crackle is drying, mix mustard paint for the top coat as above. Brush mustard paint over the crackle medium, following the wood grain (see photo). Do not paint over the same area twice or you may disturb the crackling, which forms as the paint dries. The paint consistency determines the crack size; the thicker the paint, the larger the cracks. Be careful not to apply too much paint or cracks will not appear at all. Let dry. Seal with clear matte sealer.

MILK PAINT *Crackle*

SOFTENED COLOR

INSTEAD OF BANISHING a brightly painted chair to the basement or kid's room, make it into a sophisticated accent. Use a tinted antiquing glaze and light distressing to soften raucous color schemes and evoke a gently aged appeal. We started with a chair painted in vivid blue, aqua, green and yellow. Lightly sand the surface and wipe with a tack cloth. Brush on a coat of mushroom-hued glaze to visually link the different colors and give the piece a grayish tone. Apply the glaze to one area at a time, brushing in the direction of the wood grain. Concentrate thicker coats of glaze around decorative turnings and joints. Let the glaze sit for a minute, then lightly wipe off excess to create brighter highlighted areas. Buff glaze from heavily coated areas with fine steel wool, then lightly sand portions to partially reveal previously painted layers. When your new touched-by-time finish is complete, protect it with a coat of clear matte sealer.

BEFORE

Index

Sources

Pages 20-21
Shaper tools: Colour Shaper tools, Royal Sovereign; www.colourshaper.com; available through Dick Blick Art Materials; call 800-828-4548 or visit www.dickblick.com.

Pages 34-37, 112
Glass paints: PermEnamel Surface Conditioner, AirDry PermEnamels, and AirDry Satin Glaze, Delta Technical Coatings; call 800-423-4135 or visit www.deltacrafts.com.

Pages 40-41
Spray stain: Design Master Home Decor Stain, Design Master; call 800-525-2644 or visit www.dmcolor.com.

Pages 42-43
Oil pencils: Oil-Colour package of 36 colors, Walnut Hollow, call 800-950-5101 or visit www.walnuthollow.com.

Page 51
Wood-burning tool: Creative Versa-Tool, Walnut Hollow, as above.

Pages 54-55
Veneer and adhesive: PaperWood paper-thin veneers and pressure-sensitive adhesive Lenderink Technologies, Inc.; call 616-887-8257 or visit www.lenderink.com.

Pages 56-57, 76-77
Frosted glass spray finish: Frosted Glass Finish, Krylon; call 800-4-KRYLON or visit www.krylon.com.

Pages 58-59
Etching cream and stencils: Armour Etch Glass Etching Cream and Peel N Etch Stencils, Etchworld; call 800-872-3458 or visit www.etchworld.com.

Pages 84-85, 96
Imprints and imprint adhesive: Custom Imprints, Imprint Coat, Faux Effects International; call 800-270-8871 or visit www.fauxfx.com.

Pages 88, 104-105
Floral spray paint: Design Master Color Tool, Design Master; as above.

Pages 90-91, 97
Heat tool: Creative Versa-Tool, Walnut Hollow, as above.

Pages 94-95, 97
Image transfer paper: Waterslide decal transfer paper, Lazertran; call 800-245-7547 or visit www.lazertran.com.

Pages 120-121
Rottenstone: Rotten Stone by Rainbow, Rockler Woodworking and Hardware; call 800-279-4441 or visit www.rockler.com.

Pages 125
Milk paint and crackle medium: Salem Red and Mustard milk paint and Antique Crackle, The Old Fashioned Milk Paint Co.; call 866-350-6455 or visit www.milkpaint.com.

Credits

PROJECT DESIGNERS:

Bob Clark, Christy Crafton, Jamie Dean, Debbie Egizio, Marge Jackson, Mike Karambelas, Maureen Looney, Mike Morris, Michelle Rosales, Carol Schalla, Seneca Simmons, Erin Vokoun

Find Great
Do-It-Yourself
Projects All Year Long

Subscribe to *Country Sampler Decorating Ideas*

Direct from the editors of *Furniture Fix-ups*, *Country Sampler Decorating Ideas* will help you create the home of your dreams. With each issue featurin up-to-the-minute home fashions, hot color combinations, new products, free patterns and step-by-step photography, it's the magazine designed to make you a success.

In Every Issue
- Picture-perfect paint proje
- Step-by-step instructions
- Decorating techniques
- Budget-friendly makeovers
- Space-stretching strategie
- Trash-to-treasure revivals
- Can-do designs for real peo

To subscribe, call 800-678-9717 or visit our Web site at www.sampler.com today!

PRACTICE WORKSHEETS

Claro que sí!

SECOND EDITION

RUSCH

CAYCEDO GARNER